Monographs on Archaeology and the Fine Arts

Sponsored by

The Archaeological Institute of America

and

The College Art Association of America

MONOGRAPH XVI Editor, *Bates Lowry*

The publication of this monograph has been aided

by a grant from the Samuel H. Kress Foundation

THE MURALS OF EUGENE DELACROIX AT SAINT-SULPICE

JACK J. SPECTOR RUTGERS UNIVERSITY

The College Art Association of America   New York, New York

1967

Copyedited by *Jean Lilly*   Designed by *Malcolm Grear*

Printed by *The Meriden Gravure Co.*

Library of Congress Catalog Card Number: 67-30384

PREFACE

There is little doubt in my mind that what is needed most urgently for nineteenth century scholarship is a series of monographs treating key works deeply and in many aspects. Up to now most good writings on nineteenth century art have handled their subjects on the one hand in books surveying many artists or many works of one artist, and on the other hand in articles discussing a few aspects of one work. This study of Delacroix's murals at Saint-Sulpice combines both approaches and so bridges a gap, for it discusses at length and from many viewpoints a very important group of paintings and places these paintings in the broad context of their time.

The subject of this monograph crystallized as a dissertation topic several years ago in conversations with Professor Meyer Schapiro at Columbia University; however, my interest in the great Romantic's art—mainly in its more violent aspects—began long before, in childhood. My initial impression when standing in front of Delacroix's murals was therefore somewhat of a letdown; for, contrary to my expectations, I found that the celebrated colorist's decorations seemed relatively gray. Actually, the exciting qualities of the murals, then lying under the veil of a Paris winter (and doubtless less brilliant than in their pristine condition) were not to be revealed until springtime. In the brighter sunlight of that season, the jeweled colors of some parts of the murals sparkled with remarkable richness and recalled the Delacroix I had first admired.

In preparing the dissertation upon which much of the present book is based, I incurred a number of debts, which I wish gratefully to acknowledge. The grant of a University Fellowship by Columbia University in 1959-1960 permitted me to lay the groundwork for my research by reading about Delacroix's mural paintings at Saint-Sulpice and elsewhere. The next year, 1960-1961, a Fulbright Fellowship to Paris enabled me to study the murals at first hand. During the years 1961-1963, when I undertook the difficult labor of assembling the mass of my materials, I often applied the superb methodology of Professor Julius S. Held, with which I became familiar in several seminars. Professor Held and Professor Theodore Reff made helpful suggestions on the dissertation in the final stages. Professor Rudolf Wittkower kindly offered valuable suggestions on my rough draft. Most of all I am indebted to Professor Meyer Schapiro, my adviser, who illuminated many perplexing problems of style and content. Indirectly through his lectures and seminars and directly in our conversations, Professor Schapiro guided my work with unfailing generosity.

In revising the dissertation as a book I benefited from the perceptive criticisms of my colleagues Professor A. Carter Jefferson and Professor Martin Eidelberg. Grants from the Rutgers Research Council helped me to continue my postdoctoral work, and to provide the book with illustrations. The watchful eyes of Jean Lilly, who read the proof, saved the book from a number of mistakes.

Publication of this monograph was made possible above all by the support of the Kress Foundation.

Columbia University's Fine Arts Library was especially valuable to me because of its excellent staff, including the late Miss M. W. Chamberlin and Miss E. F. Wedge, at that time her assistant. In Paris I was fortunate enough to receive help from M. Jean Adhémar, chief curator of the Cabinet des Estampes, B. N.; from Mlles. Bacou and Giot of the Cabinet des Dessins, Louvre; from Mlles. Bataille and Barbin of the Bibliothèque Doucet, Institut d'Art et d'Archéologie; and from the staffs of the Archives Nationales and of the Archives de la Seine. The prompt and informative replies to my letters by museum curators (to whom I am grateful, but who are too numerous to mention here) gave me indispensable aid in gathering Delacroix's preparatory drawings for his murals at Saint-Sulpice.

To Professor H. W. Janson, who first accepted my manuscript for publication in the Monograph Series, I owe a debt of gratitude for helpful suggestions. I am also grateful to Professor Bates Lowry, who in mid-course succeeded Professor Janson to editorship of the Monograph Series and who has contributed generous and sensitive guidance to the book's publication.

My wife Helga's understanding and warm interest contributed greatly to the completion of this book.   J.J.S.

CONTENTS

Eugène Delacroix, *Heliodorus Driven from the Temple* (detail). Paris, Saint-Sulpice, Chapelle des Saints-Anges, 1849-61
(photo: Le Temps/M. Lavrillier for Maurice Sérullaz, *Les peintures murales de Delacroix*, Paris: Editions du Temps, 1963)

INTRODUCTION

The great decorations by Eugène Delacroix (1798-1863) at Saint-Sulpice are an exception to the generally uninventive and traditional church painting produced in France in the middle of the nineteenth century. They were completed at a time when contemporary critics, deploring the low quality of religious painting, offered various suggestions for its revival. The Catholic Church itself paid more attention to censorship than to the production and preservation of religious art: it required the stimulation of lay critics interested in archaeology and aesthetic questions to compel the Church to attend to the artistic losses caused by deterioration and theft.[1]

This apparent apathy in matters of direct concern to the Church derived in part from the deep-going changes brought about by the Revolution of 1789, after which the Church often had to follow the lead of the State. At such times Catholicism was both confined to nonpolitical areas and promoted by the government as an extension of its own powers. In the tradition of Napoleon I's *Concordat*, Napoleon III, anxious about the instability of his regime, spoke of religion as a means of maintaining order among the populace. Governmental patronage of the arts—secular and religious—was another technique for retaining sympathy, and the government supported the Universal Exhibition of 1855. The churches, long regarded as national monuments, were renovated with numerous restorations and decorations, including Delacroix's work carried out in a chapel at Saint-Sulpice, Paris, from 1849 to 1861.

The three paintings comprising the project have with reason been termed the summit of Delacroix's art, and—as his last major work—his artistic "testament."[2] Some critics have even compared the chapel's significance for Parisian artists to that of the Brancacci chapel for Florentine artists.[3]

N.B. A bibliography of important sources, given short titles in the footnotes, follows the Appendices. Abbreviations: *Art Bulletin—AB; Burlington Magazine—BurlM; Gazette des Beaux-Arts—GBA; JWarb—Journal of the Warburg and Courtauld Institutes.*

1. See Paul Frankl, *The Gothic*, Princeton, 1960, 519, for a discussion of Arcisse de Caumont (1801-73), whose "main achievement was to unite all architects, archaeologists, clergymen and the like who were interested in the preservation of medieval objects...." Cf. also Mgr. Baunard, *Un siècle de l'église de France 1800-1900*, Paris, 1901, 241.

2. See Maurice Barrès, "Le testament d'Eugène Delacroix," *Revue hebdomadaire*, VI, 3 (June 18, 1921), 249-60 (reprinted in *Le mystère en pleine lumière*, Paris, 1926, 108-16; Fernand Vallon, *Au Louvre avec Delacroix*, Grenoble, 1930, Intro. by Elie Faure, xii; Paul Jamot, Preface to *L'oeuvre décoratif d'Eugène Delacroix au Palais du Luxembourg, Exposition* (May 15-30), Paris, 1936; and G. Charensol, "De la Rue de Furstenberg au Palais Bourbon," *Revue des deux mondes*, October 1, 1957, 540. Lucien Rudrauf develops Barrès's interpretation in his "De la bête à l'ange (Les étapes de la lutte vitale dans la pensée et l'art d'Eugène Delacroix)," *Acta Historiae Artium*, IX, 1963, 3-4, pp. 295-341, esp. 340-41.

3. See Julius Meier-Graefe, *Modern Art*, London, 1908 (2 vols.), trans. F. Simmonds and G. W. Chrystal, I, 152; Walter Pach, *The Classical Tradition in Modern Art*, New York, 1959, 28.

1 View toward the west wall of the Chapelle des Saints-Anges. Paris, Saint-Sulpice (photo: Agraci)

The Chapelle des Saints-Anges, which contains Delacroix's murals, lies next to the south tower of Saint-Sulpice. One enters it most directly via Place Saint-Sulpice (with its fountain completed in 1847 by Visconti). Passing through the Italianate west portal added by Servandoni to the church in 1733-1749, the visitor may turn right directly after entering and confront the celebrated chapel (Fig. 1). A round-arched window in the south wall provides the main light, and some additional light from the nave comes through the chapel's north entrance. Left and right of the window two paintings of equal size (23½′ x 15½′) and of the same shape as the window face each other, and a third painting, oval in shape (measuring 16⅖′ major axis x 12½′ minor axis), looks down on the room from the ceiling. The two works below are painted directly on the wall in an oil and wax medium, whereas the ceiling is an oil on canvas, glued to the wall (marouflage).[4]

The left or east wall contains Delacroix's painting *Jacob Wrestling with the Angel* (Fig. 2), which shows two figures at the left wrestling amid striking green foliage, and numerous smaller figures in a caravan at the right. The theme comes from *Genesis* 24:9, which tells how Jacob, alone beside the river Jabbok, met an angel of the Lord, with whom he wrestled all night. The angel, at the approach of daybreak, when he had to leave, had still not overcome Jacob, and—as in Delacroix's painting—touched Jacob's thigh, laming him. But Jacob refused to let the angel go, demanding a blessing first. The angel then renamed him "Israel," or one who had striven with God and with men and had prevailed.

The right or west wall contains Delacroix's golden-gray painting, *Heliodorus Driven from the Temple* (Fig. 3), showing a fallen warrior punished by three angels, one of them on horseback, at the entrance to the Temple of Jerusalem. The theme comes from II *Maccabees* 3:1-393, which describes an incident that occurred during the reign of Seleucus IV Philopator (187-175 B.C.), the Hellenistic ruler who—at least in the version known to Delacroix—dispatched his officer Heliodorus to plunder the Temple of Jerusalem. While he and his guards were perpetrating this sacrilege in front of the treasury, Onias, the high priest, and all the people were praying to God with hands upraised to heaven. Suddenly, miraculously, the apparition of the horseman and two whipping angels sent by God intervened to save the treasure and punish Heliodorus.

The ceiling is decorated with the familiar theme of *St. Michael Vanquishing Lucifer* (Fig. 4), a subject based on the episode in the Revelation of St. John 12:7-9.

---

4. The technique of the ceiling has sometimes—incorrectly—been called true fresco. Meier-Graefe, thinking that Robaut meant true fresco by the word *fresque*, offered his own mistaken description of the murals as tempera. See Meier-Graefe, *Eugène Delacroix. Beiträge zu einer Analyse*, Munich, 1922: p. 59, and especially p. 66, describes the whole decoration of the murals as fresco, and says that he prefers to call them "tempera." The term *fresque* was actually current among 19th century French writers to designate any mural painting, and the oil-wax medium was often wrongly called *encaustique*, although the colors were not applied to the surface with heat. See "Peintures à fresque. Exécutées par M. J. Jollivet dans l'Eglise Saint-Ambroise-Popincourt," *L'artiste*, 3rd ser., 4, 1843, 353-57 (signed "A.F.").

5. For a typical example of more recent praise of Delacroix's chapel paintings for their high re-

2 Delacroix, *Jacob Wrestling with the Angel*. Paris, Saint-Sulpice, Chapelle des Saints-Anges (photo: Agraci)

3 Delacroix, *Heliodorus Driven from the Temple*. Paris, Saint-Sulpice, Chapelle des Saints-Anges (photo: Agraci)

Delacroix's commission is doubly remarkable: it was given to a man known for unorthodox religious views; and he succeeded so well in this epoch of feeble religious painting that now, over one hundred years later, some Catholic writers consider his paintings great religious art.[5] But to Delacroix the thrill and challenge of his church decoration had nothing to do with religious sentiment; rather, he strove to emulate the genius of the older masters he admired (Raphael, Titian, Rubens), who had treated either the same or comparable subjects.

Initially, few critics praised the religious quality of the murals, whose dramatic movement appeared excessive and hardly capable of the calming effect expected from a church decoration. Ecclesiastical censors, who regarded stylistic innovations as unorthodox, favored attempts to recover old and sanctified technical processes; they especially preferred fresco to oil on canvas, as more consonant with the architecture and thus providing a means for the walls to dominate the painting.[6] The intention was to minimize the artist's aggressive self-expression, more and more patent in religious as well as in secular painting since the High Renaissance. Inevitably such critics would object to a church decoration such as Delacroix's, which was so exciting and which displayed in their eyes more art than piety.

After the era of Napoleon I, the Church's jurisdiction over the decoration of its own walls was conditioned by the fact that the government paid the bills. It became increasingly difficult for the artist, upon whom divergent claims by Church and State were being made, to decorate churches with the naive intensity attributed to earlier Christian artists. In their quest for such artists many Catholic writers turned willingly from the controversial productions of Delacroix to the placid linear art of Hippolyte Flandrin, a "modern Fra Angelico" who embodied the pious qualities which they regarded as supremely present in the Italian Quattrocento. The models of Christian faith and religious art were sought in epochs far from the secular modern era: purity meant remoteness in time.

Historicizing was in the air: thus Delacroix's *Heliodorus* was praised by some writers above Raphael's on certain points of archaeological exactness. Romanticism coupled this interest in the archaic to a taste for the exotic. Delacroix, who joined an expedition sent by Louis-Philippe to Africa, found there—as contemporary and earlier Frenchmen had—living images of the ancient Romans and the biblical patriarchs.[7] In the late 1840's and early 1850's the widespread enthusiasm for classical and Jewish antiquity in France affected painting, poetry and the theater,

ligious quality despite the artist's skepticism, see Maurice Denis, "Etat actuel de l'art religieux," *GBA*, 2nd ser., 10, 1933, 57, and Joseph Pichard, *L'art sacré moderne*, Paris, 1953, 16.

6. This censorious attitude was typical of Catholic art criticism of the 1850's, and such writers as the Abbé Gaume and Didron the elder, among others, militantly denounced "paganism in Christian art." The great Seicento painters were especially decried by the more extreme critics for their "pagan sensualism" and their lack of a genuinely religious motivation. See Abbé J. Gaume, *Le ver rongeur des sociétés modernes, ou le paganisme dans l'education*, Paris, 1851, 22; and Didron the elder, *Le paganisme dans l'art chrétien*, Paris, 1853, 10.

7. Pre-revolutionary explorations in Asia Minor and Africa had already sought living models of the original biblical patriarchs in their modern descendants, and when Napoleon I conducted his

4 Delacroix, *St. Michael Vanquishing Lucifer*. Paris, Saint-Sulpice, Chapelle des Saints-Anges (photo: Agraci)

leading to the success of Couture's *Romans of the Decadence* (1847) on the one hand and of Chassériau's *Susanna and the Elders* (1839) on the other, to which Théophile Gautier in 1852 applied the epithet: "The beauty of Israel ennobled by the art of Greece."[8] The great Romantic Delacroix, who vividly imagined classical, mediaeval and Renaissance, as well as Oriental and African themes, based his art as much on his own perceptions as on literature and fantasy; indeed, for his decoration of the chapel he drew on experiences not only in Africa, but near Paris, where in a forest not far from Barbizon he studied oak trees for the landscape of his *Jacob*.

Curiosity about the arts of other times and places was accompanied by open-minded experimentation in all media; hence the attempt to discover a technique of mural painting which would be permanent in the unfavorable climatic conditions of French winters. The idea of using an oil and wax medium, which had already been esteemed in the eighteenth century in France and England, was revived in 1829 by Paillot de Montabert in a book and earlier in his paintings exhibited at the Salons.[9] Delacroix could have been inspired by any one of these sources to try out the technique on his first large-scale mural decoration, that of the Salon du Roi (1833), and ultimately at Saint-Sulpice.[10]

On all of his great mural projects Delacroix worked with helpers, whom he trained to perform the intermediary tasks of preparing the backgrounds and ornaments of the murals while he usually devoted himself to the two tasks he much preferred: at the start, working out the composition (and the color), which he often sketched on the wall; and at the end retouching the nearly completed painting. Clearly such a procedure makes it difficult to determine which hand executed a given detail. The criterion of quality assures us only that whatever is brilliantly painted is from the master's hand, but it is not decisive for the less important passages. Another guide would be an acquaintance with the helpers' styles, very difficult to discover for the more obscure among them, but possible for the two assistants at Saint-Sulpice, both of whom exhibited at the Salons. Louis Boulangé, a landscapist acquainted with stage design, was given less conspicuous background areas to fill in; whereas Pierre Andrieu, the more skilled, was valued

military campaign in Egypt, he drew France's attention to this "biblical land." An interest was revived again in 1822 by Champollion's deciphering of the hieroglyphs. For a comparison of the architecture of the ancient Athenians and modern Orientals, see J. J. Hittorff, *Restitution du Temple d'Empedocle à Selinonte, ou l'architecture polychrome chez les Grecs*, Paris, 1851, 616 n. 1; see also E. Fromentin, *Lettres de jeunesse*, 3rd ed., Paris, 1909, 187, letter of 1846. The romantic painter Horace Vernet, who had been to Africa in the army as early as 1814, read a memoir to the Académie des Beaux-Arts in 1847 entitled "Opinion sur certains rapports qui existent entre les costumes des anciens Hébreux et celui des Arabes

modernes." Cf. Chassériau's letter of 1846 on the Jews and Arabs of Algeria, in Léonce Bénédite, *Chassériau*, Paris, 1931, 271. For other details, see Léon Rosenthal, *Du romantisme au réalisme*, Paris, 1914, 90-92.

8. For a list of some of the paintings, poems and plays produced at this time, see Bénédite, *Chassériau*, 423. Gautier's remark is in his *Salon de 1852*, and is cited in Bénédite, *Chassériau*, 403.

9. See Paillot de Montabert, *Traité complet de la peinture*, Paris, 1829, viii. The article cited in note 4 above, "Peintures à fresque...," *L'artiste*, 3rd ser., 4, 1843, 353-57 (signed "A.F.") pointed out (p. 355) that "M. de Montabert has had the honor of restoring the practice" of the technique,

by Delacroix sufficiently to have been entrusted with more prominent details. The contribution of Andrieu may be better defined when a recently discovered diary for 1852 is published. From a brief study of this diary in the summer of 1964, I concluded that it was the helper's notebook for his work at Saint-Sulpice.[11]

Delacroix's paintings at Saint-Sulpice, both in their importance and in their complexity demand the closest study; yet writings about them have until now not gone beyond assembling relevant facts. In the succeeding chapters of this book I will take up and discuss at length the following questions:

First, under what circumstances did the skeptical Delacroix not only receive a church mural decoration, but produce the most interesting and important religious painting of his time?

Second, how did Delacroix's compositional ideas evolve, and what were the steps of the long development from the first hints of the commission in 1847 to its completion in 1861? In answering these questions I will discuss 59 sketches and drawings for the murals (plus three copies by pupils) as well as relevant portions of the artist's diary and correspondence.

Third, what artists influenced Delacroix's style, technique and subject matter at Saint-Sulpice? and what was the impact of such major issues as romanticism and Orientalism? In considering these questions I will carefully analyze the color and composition of the three murals as part of a broad tradition.

Fourth, what were the attitudes of Delacroix's contemporaries toward his chapel decorations as evidenced by their published criticism?

which had become "familiar to many painters."

10. Frédéric Villot, in his *Catalogue de la vente des tableaux...par E. Delacroix* (February 11, 1865), Paris, 1865, claimed that he taught the artist to use the medium just before he began his murals at the Salon du Roi. If so, it is most likely that the knowledgeable Villot had read of it in Paillot's book. Andrieu's discussion of Delacroix's use of the medium at the Salon du Roi to insure permanence, was published in *La Galerie Bruyas*, by Alfred Bruyas et al. (Paris, 1876). Lassalle-Bordes, in "Nouvelles notes reçues de M. Lassalle-Bordes le 16 9re 1880" (MS 245, Institut d'Art et d'Archéologie, Paris), stated that Delacroix got the idea from Reynolds. I believe that Reynolds

got it from Count Caylus. Anxieties about the deterioration of Raphael's frescoes in the Vatican led in the 18th century to efforts to copy them in such media as encaustic on canvas and mosaic. See Jacques Guillerme, "La naissance au XVIIIe s. du sentiment de responsabilité collective dans la conservation," *GBA*, 6th ser., 65, 1965, 154-62.

11. The *Agenda* of 1852 is MS 84 at the Institut d'Art et d'Archéologie, Paris. Mlle. Damiron, *conservateur* at the Institute, plans to publish it in full. For further details, see Chapter II. A precedent for the *Agenda* is in the published notes of Delacroix's helper from 1838 to 1847 at the library of the Palais Bourbon, Louis de Planet (1804-77), *Souvenirs*, Intro. and notes by A. Joubin.

I. THE COMMISSION: A SKEPTIC PAINTS A RELIGIOUS MURAL

It was above all from the standpoint of an artist that Delacroix viewed religious decoration; and among those—including artists, critics and state officials—who he hoped would attend the chapel's opening on July 31, 1861, no clergymen were mentioned.[1] In a famous passage Baudelaire praised Delacroix's religious painting as an aspect of a many-sided imagination and for its artistic, rather than for its religious, content: "The imagination of Delacroix! *That* never shrank from mounting the difficult heights of religion; heaven belongs to it, just as hell, as war, as Olympus, as sensuous pleasures. Here indeed, we have the model of the painter-poet."[2] A more common attitude—the kind against which this apology might have been directed—was that Delacroix had too nervous a temperament to produce good religious art, and that his aim "to impress his personality on his works" conflicted with that of the true religious painter, to glorify God;[3] indeed, another critic referred to his art as "pictorial Protestantism," implying that his strong individualism bordered on rebelliousness.[4]

Delacroix's attitude toward religion (one variant of an attitude underlying the beliefs of other contemporaries, e.g. Lamartine, Hugo, Vigny among the poets, and his friend Chenavard among the painters) is not a committed atheism, nor a faith made visible in moments of stress, as some religious apologists feel;[5] in fact, he wrote to George Sand on November 25, 1860: "What shall we find beyond? Night, fearful night. There is nothing better in store for us; that, at least, is what I sadly feel." For comfort he turned to the Stoic Marcus Aurelius' book as a "consoling religion of resignation."[6]

1. For valuable criticism of this chapter, I owe debts of gratitude to Professor Jean-Albert Bédé of Columbia and to my colleague, Professor Alfred Carter Jefferson. For Delacroix's criticism of religious decorations on purely aesthetic grounds, see the *Journal*, April 2 and April 5, 1852. The invitations are discussed below, Chapter II, B. See also the letter to Delacroix's friend Riesener, Sept. 1, 1861.

2. See Baudelaire's "Salon of 1859," in *The Mirror of Art*, New York, 1956. For similar evaluations of Delacroix's religious painting by other writers, some of them earlier, see the important book by Lucie Horner, *Baudelaire, critique de Delacroix*, Paris, 1956, and in addition see below, Appendix III. Théophile Silvestre, in *Les artistes français*, Brussels, 1861, 30, remarked that "Delacroix is consumed with a thirst for immortality, with an air of skepticism," and on p. 31 explained that he viewed the decoration of the chapel as offering Delacroix a chance "to leave one more masterpiece on the durable walls of a monument." In

their tradition of high rhetoric, members of the Académie Française have discussed Delacroix's murals, especially the *Jacob*, finding in it a theme of personal and artistic heroism; see, e.g., L. Hourticq, "Eugène Delacroix," *Revue de l'art ancien et moderne*, January 1930, 3-12, and R. Huyghe, *Delacroix*, Paris, 1963.

3. See Olivier Merson, "La Chapelle des Saints-Anges à Saint-Sulpice par M. Eugène Delacroix," *Revue contemporaine*, March 15, 1862, 162f.

4. See E. J. Delécluze, "Salon de 1848," *Revue de Paris*, June 1848, 155-86. Cf. Abbé J. Gaume's remark in *Le ver rongeur . . .*, 21, "Lucifer was the first Protestant."

5. Cf. Barrès, "Le testament d'Eugène Delacroix," 108-16. On Chenavard, see Joseph C. Sloane, *Chenavard, Artist of 1848*, Chapel Hill, 1962.

6. See the *Journal* (ed. Joubin), March 11, 1847. Delacroix referred several times to the great Stoic, and painted the important *Death of Marcus Aurelius* for the Salon of 1845.

Delacroix's words "Dieu est en nous," written near the end of his life, probably come from Ovid, and precede a discussion of "genius" and "inspiration," which meant for him the gift of creative ability, and above all, the fusion of his sense of identity with belief in his creative powers.[7] Whereas the Christian grounds his identity and individuality in a faith that God exists and is the superior source or agent of all his energies, Delacroix longed to be like God as a man and as an artist.

Painting was for Delacroix an exhilarating release of creative energies, which often carried him beyond his fellow artists. Indeed, he first became famous by shocking his contemporaries with his daring treatment of themes such as the *Massacre of Scio* (1824), with its display of butchered women and children; *The Death of Sardanapalus* (1827), where an Assyrian king surveys the slaughter of his harem and the destruction of his prized possessions as a prelude to suicide; and numerous animal hunts and combats red with spilling blood. Throughout his career, the biblical themes he chose to illustrate were mainly theatrical and dramatic. It was never maintained that Delacroix painted violent scenes out of a tortured religious imagination, like a latter-day Jean Duvet (1485-1561),[8] for apart from the predominantly secular character of his work, he was noted for his very lucid mind and for an attitude toward religion marked more by skepticism than by faith. Nevertheless, Delacroix, like the orthodox and staid H. Flandrin, was given a church commission. Almost a century later, the Catholic historian R. Aubert, regretfully contemplating the art of this period, observed: "...one had the choice between some beautiful works, whose title alone distinguishes them from profane art (such as Delacroix's *Heliodorus*), and some dull evangelical scenes without artistic value...."[9] We may well wonder why and how Delacroix received his commission.

In the Introduction I outlined the situation in mid-nineteenth century France which resulted in Delacroix's receiving from the State rather than from the Church itself his commission to decorate Saint-Sulpice. I pointed out that this was an instance of the State's financial control of the Church. I now want to discuss more precisely the role of religious art in this situation and, in particular, the role of Delacroix's religious painting prior to his Saint-Sulpice commission.[10]

7. See the *Journal*, October 12, 1862. The sentence following "God is within us..." reads: "It is he [i.e., God; Pach mistranslates *lui* as 'that'] who inspires men of genius and warms them with the spectacle of their own productions." The whole passage seems to derive from the celebrated phrase in Ovid's *Fasti* 6.5: *Est deus in nobis, agitante calescimus illo*. In the Loeb Library translation the passage reads: "There is a god within us. It is when he stirs us that our bosom warms; it is his impulse that sows the seeds of inspiration," etc. Delacroix admired the Roman poet, from whom he derived the themes of several paintings. A similar phrase can be found in a novel by his old friend and legatee, George Sand, *Spiridion*, ca. 1839, vol. 34 in the Calmann-Lévy edition of her works (Paris, n.d.). On p. 431 occurs the phrase "Dieu est en vous" in connection with man's divinity, to be realized in a future blending of all religions, when Plato will stand beside Jesus.

8. Delacroix admired this remarkable engraver.

9. R. Aubert, "Le pontificat de Pie IX, 1846-78," *Histoire de l'église*, XXI, 1952.

With the Revolution and the mass exodus of priests, for a time Catholicism and, consequently, religious decoration practically disappeared from view. When Napoleon I, recognizing its persistent influence, legalized Catholicism, he was able to use papal authority to place the French church under his own authority. The Concordat of 1801 made the Church a protected dependent of the State, not the basis for a state religion, although it recognized Catholicism as "the religion of the majority of Frenchmen."

The Catholic renaissance signaled by Chateaubriand failed to inspire a new art to refurbish church walls stripped by the patriots; moreover, government patronage for monumental decoration was given to the nonreligious David and his followers. This failure to produce a new religious art is not surprising. A steady decrease in the number of commissions for church decorations began with the decline of church building in the late seventeenth century. Besides, the combination of devoutness and artistic talent of men like Lesueur and Philippe de Champaigne in the seventeenth century became increasingly rare in the eighteenth century, when a spirit of enlightened skepticism prevailed.[11] Those few artists who still painted noteworthy religious decoration in the eighteenth century were either survivors of the past century (François le Moyne) or the last members of an exhausted school (Doyen). Often, in this century dominated by Boucher and Fragonard, a pleasantly sensuous art decorated the churches (Charles Eisen). The grave and uninspired art of Vien, reacting against his master Natoire's frivolous virtuosity, seemed to some to point toward a renewed tradition of religious art, but in fact it led in a very different direction, to the secular Neoclassicism of his pupil David. Some writers, following Mme. de Staël, declared that both religion and art were on the verge of disappearing.

Mme. de Staël had announced the end of religious art too soon. While Napoleon I's official support of Catholicism in the wake of the Revolution was flauntingly cynical and arbitrary, the religious pomp of the Bourbon Restoration of 1815-1830, with its Gallican Church, was both craftier and more significant.[12] An official of the Chamber of Deputies in 1832 summed up the distinction between the roles played by art in the two periods: "In the Empire, art was fawning, in the Restoration it became at the same time fawning and sanctimonious."[13] The styles of the two epochs differed accordingly. Napoleon's artists, rejecting the charmingly undignified decorative art of the eighteenth century, produced stately secular works in their studios with small regard for the decorative role, often without even knowing which walls the paintings were to

10. Adrien Dansette, *Histoire religieuse de la France contemporaine de la révolution à la 3e république*, Paris, 1948, discusses French Catholicism with great clarity and accuracy, and should be consulted for the rest of this chapter.

11. See Louis Réau, *Le rayonnement de Paris au 18ème siècle*, Paris, 1946, 99. For the opposite view that there was by no means a decline of religious art during the 18th century in Paris, see

Louis Dimier, *L'église et l'art*, Paris, 1935, esp. pp. 228-40.

12. The Gallicans were French Catholics with Royalist sympathies who favored strengthening the national church through its bishops, and the limitation of papal power. Their opponents, the Ultramontanists, wished to concentrate all the powers of the Church in the hands of the Pope.

13. Cited by Rosenthal, *Du romantisme*, 8.

cover.[14] When the grand rhetoric of Napoleon's time was silenced, Restoration artists, less obtrusive than their revolutionary forebears, became concerned that their church murals should be fitting ornaments for the architecture.

With the return of the Bourbons and the resumption of church building, religious painting was revived as a genre conducive to spiritual tranquillity; for Napoleon's successors, the Bourbon kings of the Restoration, sought peace and order in all things. In church mural painting this was to be secured by a cautious and calm propriety. Fresco—already regarded during the Revolution as the best technique for monumental decorations[15]—seemed nicely adapted to the new needs of Restoration art, and Italy, long considered by French artists—sometimes grudgingly—the proper home of the medium, resumed the role of teacher.[16] The frescoes of Raphael were extolled as exemplary, and when in 1822 a pamphlet discussed Vinchon's recent frescoes (in the same year as the frescoes painted at Saint-Sulpice by Pujol, David's pupil) in a chapel at Saint-Sulpice, the very process was shown to be superior to that of oil by a reference to the fresco coloring of Raphael's *Heliodorus*.[17]

However, because there were not enough good artists skilled in fresco technique, and especially because past experience had shown that frescoes weathered poorly in the cold damp climate of Paris winters, the medium was used infrequently; indeed, throughout the nineteenth century, from as early as 1812, it was common practice for the City of Paris and the State to commission canvases for church decoration.[18]

The question of what could constitute religious art, considering the loss of iconographic traditions, puzzled the unhappy Delécluze, writing in 1824-1828:[19] "The epoch of the Restoration and of the exile of David was a great mishap for the arts. They tried to employ the talents of artists to make paintings for the Church. This attempt succeeded neither for the government nor for the artists. The traditions of figural types and of costumes for the sacred characters were

14. Cf. Rosenthal, *Du romantisme*, 299, which notes that Napoleon, following the vagaries of his time, commissioned the *Distribution of Eagles* and the *Sacre* from David, without knowing where he would place them.
15. See F. Benoit, *L'art français sous la révolution et l'empire. Les doctrines. Les idées. Les genres*, Paris, 1897, 420.
16. Mural artists usually visited Rome or Florence to complete their education. See Benoit, *L'art français*, 213.
17. See *Notice sur les peintures à fresque exécutées à Saint-Sulpice dans la chapelle de Saint-Maurice par Auguste Vinchon*, Paris, 1822, a copy of which is in the Cabinet des Estampes, No. Yb³/688.
18. For the point that there were more frescoes painted under the *ancien régime* with its costly tastes in decoration than under post-Revolution-

ary governments, see Rosenthal, *Du romantisme*, 299. In 1812 the State commissioned Gros's painting, *Charles V Received by Francis I at the Abbey of St. Denis*, for the new sacristy of Saint Denis. This basically secular work was transferred in 1823 to the Musée Royal (now in the Louvre). The City of Paris in 1823 and later years commissioned four paintings for Saint-Nicolas-des-Champs, the earliest being Léon Cogniet's *St. Stephen Helping a Poor Family*. Delacroix was commissioned in 1826 by the City of Paris to paint a canvas for Saint Paul-Saint Louis. For examples between 1840 and 1860, see Appendix I. For a good picture of the confusions resulting from the fact that commissions originated both from the City of Paris and the State, see the unsigned article "Peintures murales de la chapelle Saint-Landrie à Saint-Germain-l'Auxerrois,"

lost. One no longer knew the Christian religion save through the intermediary of Chateaubriand's writings." Indeed religious painting, less and less supported by the Bourbon government in its final crisis, again appeared on the verge of extinction as an art form.[20]

The Revolution of 1830 replaced the Bourbon with Louis-Philippe's bourgeois regime, and the royalist Gallican elements of the Church, no longer supported by the State, yielded place to the Roman sympathizers. The new government at first cooperated with and supported the Church, and commissions for religious paintings multiplied. During the period just after the Revolution, when the bourgeois government adopted liberal politics, there emerged independently a strong liberal Catholicism, led by Lamennais. This tendency was tolerated by Gregory XVI and Louis-Philippe as a popular and less dangerous alternative to socialism. However, Lamennais's persistent demand that the State relinquish all control over the education of Catholics alienated him first from the King and then from the Pope, who wished to maintain good relations with Louis-Philippe. Gregory XVI soon turned against a movement which was becoming more liberal than Catholic.

With his growing power Louis-Philippe became more conservative and by 1832 surely sympathized with the Pope's campaign against liberal French Catholicism. But by the 1840's the rationalistic, anticlerical bourgeois in his government and in the opposition, exerted increasing pressure on the Church, and helped force the Pope to withdraw the Jesuits from France in 1845.[21] Pius IX, whose papacy commenced in 1846, aggravated matters by attempting to appeal to the masses of workers through liberal politics. In 1847 the mainstay of Louis-Philippe's government were the anticlerical bourgeois, whereas French Catholicism, now under the firm control of Pius IX, aimed to secure popular approval; indeed, during the February Revolution the Church, with its growing following among the workers in the provinces as well as in Paris,

L'artiste, 3rd ser., 4, 1843, 289-92, esp. 289: "For some years past, numerous works have been commissioned, some by the Minister of the Interior, others by the City of Paris. Unfortunately...these commissions have been made without agreement or unity. What the City of Paris wants often is contrary to what the Fine Arts direction wants. Also these paintings are conceived and executed according to quite different, even opposed, systems. The Minister inclines to a material representation of nature, the City of Paris to mystical forms. On top of all this disharmony, the architect of the monument puts beside these paintings an ornamentation now of a discordant richness, now of a deplorable impoverishment.... We may add that the artist can almost never obtain a lighting arrangement made intentionally for his work...."

19. See *Journal de Delécluze*, 1824-28, Intro. and notes by Robert Baschet, Paris, 1948, 481.
20. See Rosenthal, *Du romantisme*, 83.
21. In the mid-1840's, the bourgeois press attacked the Church through the vilification of its clergy. See, e.g., *Le national* (founded by Thiers), May 24, 1845. The disrespect for church property was very widespread in Paris, to judge from unpublished letters by a government official Dessalles, sent to Dumont of the Department of Public Works and to the curé of Saint-Sulpice in October 1845. In them Dessalles advised placing a fence around Saint-Sulpice to keep out the "Parisian population," through whose "vicious habits" the outside of the church was—among other things—being turned into "a public urinal." See *Archives nationales*, F[21] 1463, no. 3593, October 31, 1845.

supported the new Republic, which in its turn protected the Church.[22] After June 1848, when the Revolution was completely crushed, the Church began to turn to the bourgeois party, which welcomed an ally against the workers; and this realignment was hastened when late in 1848 Italian revolutionaries captured Rome and frightened the Pope into fleeing. The French State under Louis-Napoleon, which sent an army to Rome to restore the Pope to power, was by 1850 granting important concessions to French Catholicism. After 1848 the disenchanted Pope, realizing how dangerous for Catholicism the broadening of the Revolution could have been, became increasingly reactionary. Louis-Napoleon put this attitude to use when he attempted to police France and to keep order through the collaboration of Church and State.

It is of considerable interest for our discussion of Delacroix's commission of 1847 to see how this great political event of 1848 affected government commissions made before that date. In fact, aside from a temporary interruption of some public services, few fundamental changes were made by the workers' ephemeral victory, and February 1848 passed leaving most of the old government machinery intact. Branches of government such as public works were especially unaffected; as late as 1862 a state ordinance could still sanction a new ruling by reference to regulations of 1843, 1849 and 1851, thus spanning outwardly quite different regimes.[23]

Delacroix's commission, like those of other artists decorating churches at this time (Chassériau, Couture), was directly under government supervision.[24] Even in Louis-Philippe's administration, church *prélat* had to consult with government *préfet* concerning a program of church decoration, and once an agreement was reached, the government allowed no change.[25] This restriction helps to account for the fact that the curé at Saint-Sulpice made many changes of plan at the *outset* of negotiations, whereas after the program for the chapel had been fixed, he did not interfere again, except with Delacroix's unusual request to work on Sundays.[26]

22. Many workers remained hostile to Catholicism, and the government had to issue an order in March 1848 prohibiting the holding of popular meetings in churches.

23. See the *Archives nationales*, Paris, F²¹ 925, a note of the Ministère d'Etat concerning "travaux de bâtiments."

24. On Chassériau, see Bénédite, *Chassériau*, 177, for the prefect's specific directions to the artist on his decoration of Saint Mérry, 1842. Page 434 points out that his commission for Saint Roch, finished in 1853, came from the administration. On Couture's decoration of Saint Eustache in 1851-54, see *Thomas Couture (1815-79). Sa vie, son oeuvre*, Preface by Camille Mauclair, Paris, 1932, 34. Ingres was offered a commission by the Municipal Council to decorate a chapel in Saint-Vincent-de-Paul, but refused. See the *Revue des

beaux-arts et de la littérature par une société d'artistes et de littérateurs*, 23rd year, Paris, 1848, 12. The Prefect of the Seine had already in 1833 named a committee composed of Ingres and other famous artists to select painters to decorate chapels recently opened in Notre-Dame-de-Lorette.

25. A notice of 1844 in *Archives nationales*, F¹⁹ 7087, "Folio Budget 1841-47, Exercice 1845, chapt. x du Budget," reads: "It is forbidden ... to the ecclesiastic authorities and to the architects to execute on diocesan buildings ... any change in an approved project."

26. A famous example of the Church's successful intervention is the rejection of Chenavard's pantheistic decorations for the Pantheon after the building became a Catholic church (Sainte Geneviève), on December 6, 1851. See Sloane, *Chenavard*, 34.

Mural decoration was one of several ways in which the government rewarded the Church for its cooperation. That its generosity with regard to church decoration was wholly conditional, and that it never relinquished claims to the paintings[27] can be seen from several court cases late in the nineteenth century, when the City of Paris demanded from the Church the return of easel paintings it had paid for and given to the churches at the beginning of the century.[28]

During the period which concerns us, 1840-1860, commissions for church murals were given in Paris, either by the national or by the municipal administration. It is a striking fact that these commissions were given and worked on without interruption even before and during 1848. A list of the more important of these decorations will be found in Appendix I. The artists who executed them—Corot, Couture, Chassériau, H. Flandrin and minor pupils of Gros and Ingres—obviously did not belong to a school of Christian painting such as some Catholic writers hoped to promote.[29] However, several of Ingres's pupils employed true fresco (contrary to usual French practice), adopting Quattrocentist techniques as being most suitable for religious decoration. The vogue for this technique did not outlast the 1840's for several reasons, the chief one being (as already pointed out) its impermanence; thus, Mottez's frescoes at Saint-Germain-l'Auxerrois had to be restored less than fifteen years after they were painted.

Delacroix's friendships with influential members of the government were a powerful factor in helping him throughout his career to obtain important commissions for mural decoration.[30] Thiers, his first benefactor, secured for him the commission to decorate the Salon du Roi in the Palais Bourbon (1833-1838) and the library of the Palais Luxembourg (1840-1846). The statesman, as an important member of the opposition to Guizot's ministry, may also have helped the artist to obtain his earliest commission at Saint-Sulpice, one for the transepts. Delacroix first mentioned the transepts on January 23, 1847, and during the early months of 1847 he visited Thiers often;[31] furthermore, Baron Charles Rivet, a deputy from 1839-1846 who opposed

27. The government, ever since Napoleon I, had considered the churches not only as ecclesiastical structures but as—and sometimes only as—national monuments for whose maintenance the government was responsible.

28. See, e.g., *La lanterne*, February 20, 1891: "Un procès curieux. L'Eglise Saint-Nicolas-des-Champs et la Ville de Paris."

29. Two of the most important proponents of such projects were Alexis-François Rio, whose *De l'art chrétien* was published in 1836, and Lacordaire, who proposed a brotherhood of Christian artists in 1839. For both men, see Rosenthal, *Du romantisme*.

30. An idea of how Delacroix attempted to win commissions can be gleaned from a letter sent by him to Fr. Villot, dated August 19, 1846: "...dites-lui [Mme. Villot] que je lui ferai une peinture superbe si elle veut m'aider à intriguer auprès de M. de Rambuteau [Prefect of the Seine], auquel je voudrais tirer une carotte, et j'ai pensé que Mme. Villot, qui connaît Mme. de Rambuteau, pourrait peut-être avoir plus de succès.... Il s'agit en gros d'un petit emploi pour un pauvre hère intéressant, qui dépend dudid préfet...." But Rambuteau, who had in 1840 arranged for Delacroix to decorate a chapel at Saint-Denis-du-Saint-Sacrament (which eventuated in the *Pietà* of 1844), apparently never gave Delacroix the commission; cf. *Journal*, January 30, 1855. Charles Blanc, to whom Delacroix sent a letter of thanks "for the commission," and possibly Varcollier, head of the Division of Fine Arts, whom Delacroix also thanked in connection with Saint-Sulpice, helped directly or indirectly to get the commission for the artist.

Guizot and supported Thiers, was an old friend of Delacroix's and visited him on February 3, 1847. But the artist also seems to have made advances to Thiers's enemy Guizot, Louis-Philippe's minister, for he recorded in his *Journal* on March 6, 1847: "Mme. Guizot asks me for a sketch for a lottery. She assures me of her friendship." Since Delacroix did not keep a diary in 1846, we cannot be certain what negotiations were under way before 1847.

Following the February Revolution, the project was adjourned and not fully resumed until February 18, 1849, when the Minister of the Interior wrote to the Prefect of the Seine concerning Delacroix's commission.[32] Thiers, whose "Party of Order" gained much strength in the new Assembly, probably helped the artist very little, for—judging from the *Journal*—their friendship ended no later than February 11, 1849. Besides, Thiers's strength proved ephemeral, and he was arrested along with many republicans and royalists on December 2, 1852.

Delacroix's friend Charles Blanc, brother of the famous republican Louis Blanc, served the Second Republic as Director of Fine Arts (1848-1852). In this capacity and perhaps with the mistaken belief that Delacroix's political views were closer to his own than they actually were, he wrote a letter on April 28, 1849 to the Prefect of the Seine, praising the artist and helping to keep the commission alive through the difficult year of 1849.

Whatever his reservations, Delacroix approved the crushing of the "disorderly" February Revolution and the establishment of Louis-Napoleon's Second Republic, and readily accepted invitations from Louis not only when he was President but also when he became Emperor.[33] Delacroix cultivated Achille Fould, wealthy member of the Stock Exchange, who became Louis-Napoleon's Finance Minister on November 1, 1849.[34] Both Thiers and Fould received invitations to visit the completed chapel. Louis-Napoleon's government was quite generous to Delacroix

31. See the *Journal* entries for January 24, 26 and February 2, 3, 21, 28, 1847. A remarkable aspect of the situation is that Thiers's journal *Le national* was sharply attacking the French church at this time.

32. Another example of such interrupted projects was that of Charles Gleyre's for Saint Margaret, Paris, commissioned before 1848 and resumed on August 30, 1849. See Charles Clément, *Gleyre: Etude biographique et critique avec catalogue raisonné*, 2nd ed., Paris, 1886, 246. William S. Rubin, *Modern Sacred Art and the Church of Assy*, New York, 1961, 8, is evidently wrong when he writes: "Had there not been a Revolution of 1848, Delacroix would never have received a religious commission of such importance, and one which so discontented the increasingly defensive clergy. It was, in effect, a 'pure and unique accident' in the history of religious art." Raymond Régamey, *Eugène Delacroix. L'époque*

de la chapelle des Saints-Anges (1847-63), Paris, 1931, 146, makes the same point that the artist's commission depended on the Revolution of 1848, and also mistakenly believed that none of the earlier religious paintings were for a commission (p. 171). But, as Delacroix stated in a letter dated May 19, 1850 to Mme. Babut, this commission "is a work which I obtained under the late government, and which the revolution interrupted." Indeed, Delacroix negotiated to paint the huge transepts of the church as early as 1847.

33. See the *Journal* for February 12, 1849 and July 26, 1858. Joubin sums up Delacroix's position in 1848 succinctly with a note in the *Correspondance générale*, II, 337: "He [Delacroix] withdrew to Champrosay, where he learned with relief about Louis Napoleon's election to the Chamber on Sept. 17; he saw in that event the end of the disturbance and the return to order."

34. See the *Journal*, April 4, 1849.

and gave the artist important commissions to decorate the Gallery of Apollo at the Louvre (1850-1851) and the Salon de la Paix at the Hôtel de Ville (ca. 1850-1854).

How did Delacroix's religious painting conform to the needs of the Church and State? In answer, we may turn to Thoré's analysis of the relations of romanticism to both Church and State: "Romanticism was fundamentally so neutral *(indifférent)* a form that one could be romantic and yet...Catholic, Protestant, philosopher, absolutist, liberal, republican...."[35] While this analysis may be somewhat simplistic, it shows that it was quite understandable to some of Delacroix's contemporaries that the romantic artist should successfully conduct business both with the Church and with the State. The artist, whose work was once characterized as "color-for-color's sake"[36] (an epithet consciously derived from "art-for-art's sake"), stayed aloof from political and social issues (except in the rare instance of *Liberty Leading the People,* 1830), and never presented a deliberately anti-Catholic theme.

Delacroix painted religious themes at every phase of his career, mostly by his own choice.[37] The artist treated these themes seriously and with respect: his passion and his color are often evident here, as in his nonreligious works. He adapted his style to each subject according to its contents, without purposely distorting or injecting extraneous motifs into it, although he was sometimes unjustly accused of lapses in iconography.[38] As one might expect, the artist most successfully depicted scenes of suffering (*Christ Crucified between Two Thieves,* 1847; *The Ascent to Calvary,* 1859) or terror (*Christ on the Lake Genesaret,* 1853), whereas his occasional excursions into calmer regions (*Virgin of the Sacred Heart,* 1821; *Education of the Virgin,* 1842) are far less successful and give the feeling not so much of serene peace as of an uneasy truce.[39]

35. See the *Salons de T. Thoré, 1844-48*, Preface by W. Bürger, Paris, 1868, xxxvi. Bürger was Thoré's pseudonym. Gautier, thinking in terms of art-for-art's sake, wrote in 1839, "Great artists are always neutral *(indifférents)*." See Rosenthal, *Du romantisme*, 141.

36. See Albert Cassagne, *La théorie de l'art pour l'art en France chez les derniers romantiques et les premiers réalistes*, Paris, 1906, 101.

37. Examples of Delacroix's religious paintings are: *The Virgin of the Sacred Heart* (1821, a commission given originally to Géricault, who passed it on to Delacroix), *Christ in the Garden of Gethsemane* (1826), *The Holy Women at the Tomb* (1834), *St. Sebastian Rescued by the Holy Women* (1836), *Christ Crucified between Two Thieves* (1847), *Daniel in the Lions' Den* (1849), *The Disciples and the Holy Women Raising the Body of St. Stephen* (1853), *The Ascent to Calvary* (1859), and *Christ in the Garden of Gethsemane* (1861).

38. Thoré, e.g., criticized in his *Salon of 1847* Delacroix's *Christ Crucified between Two Thieves,* exhibited in that Salon, for having the feet of Christ nailed separately. Thoré believed that orthodox iconography required one nail. But the issue of one versus two nails was a complicated question never fully resolved, and Molanus admits both. See E. Mâle, *L'art religieux du 17ème siècle*, 270ff.

39. In her posture, and in her full-bodied, robust figure, the Virgin in the painting of 1821 has much in common with Delacroix's *Liberty* of 1830, although her attributes have been appropriately changed: the heart of Jesus in the Virgin's right hand is replaced by a tricolor flag, and the cross in her left by a rifle. It is possible that the Venus of Melos, exhibited at the Louvre in 1821, inspired the Virgin's classically posed torso.

Delacroix's religious painting prior to Saint-Sulpice—integral as it is to his oeuvre—does not constitute the most significant aspect of his art. His contemporaries, who did not actively reject his religious painting, either overlooked it or attempted to account for it in order to reconcile it with the rest of his work. Nowhere among the commissions to decorate monuments do we find religious works cited as examples of his art. Even the correspondence pertaining to the Saint-Sulpice commission cites only the decoration of the library of the Chamber of Deputies as an example of Delacroix's earlier achievements.[40] His commissions to decorate churches came from the State and were never initiated by a church official.[41]

In 1847, just at the time when negotiations for the decoration of Saint-Sulpice were starting, Thoré wrote in his *Salon* of the year:[42] "The subject is absolutely indifferent in the arts." He described Delacroix as the model of an artist working in all periods and styles, and then praised his range of subjects in words anticipating Baudelaire's, already cited: "Religion, poetry, politics, allegory, intimate and family life, he has touched them all." Delacroix's commission to paint the Chapelle des Saints-Anges would surely not have surprised Thoré.

Delacroix's commission for Saint-Sulpice depended in part (as we have seen) upon the State and its complex relations with the Church during a period marked by crisis and change. The artist's personality was a significant advantage in this situation, for his aloofness saved him from compromising political entanglements, and while his attitude of haughty disdain toward the workers and their revolution paralleled—from a loftier standpoint—the more mundane position of the state officials, it did not conflict substantially with that of church officials.[43] As an illustrious artist known to be capable of handling the difficult technical problems involved in mural decoration, Delacroix received from Louis-Philippe's government a commission which survived the 1848 Revolution into Louis-Napoleon's Republic and beyond, into Napoleon III's Empire.

40. See the *Archives nationales*, Paris, F²¹ 24, "Paris, le...184."

41. He was also commissioned to paint an oil in 1826 for the church Saint Paul-Saint Louis in Paris, *Christ in the Garden of Gethsemane*, and in 1843 the *Pietà* for Saint-Denis-du-Saint-Sacrement in Paris. In his *Journal* on January 12, 1824, Delacroix wrote of making sketches for the

Préfet, with no mention of the *curé*.

42. See the *Salon de 1847*, 447. For an even earlier anticipation of this praise of Delacroix's universality, see Maurice-Alexandre Decamps, "Salon de 1835," *Revue républicaine*, April 1835, 71. Cited in Horner, *Baudelaire*, 31.

43. Cf. letter to George Sand, May 28, 1848.

II. THE EVOLUTION OF THE MURALS

The development of Delacroix's composition can be followed partly through his sketches and partly through his *Journal* and *Correspondance,* supplemented by documents from Parisian archives. Probably the artist, who preserved and carefully edited both his literary and artistic productions, considered that the inner process thus revealed would finally contribute to a deeper appreciation of his public works. The considerable number of the surviving sketches indicates a controlled and deliberate progress; but the actual painting was tortuous and slow, delayed before it began by the relocation of the murals to be decorated and then interrupted in its course by the artist's ill health, disputes with helpers and the competing demands of concurrent projects. Moreover, Delacroix himself, troubled by a fear of impermanence in his painting (especially from humidity), protracted matters by several times having the walls scraped out and reprimed according to his precise specifications.[1]

The role of the helpers (already discussed in the Introduction) was more than perfunctory, and Andrieu in particular, to judge from his *Agenda* of 1852, may even have executed portions (exclusive of the finishing touches) of some of the major figures.[2] Indeed, some of the oil sketches are mainly by the helpers, with Delacroix's retouches. Even the finishing touches on the murals, though under the master's guidance, were sometimes left to the hand of a helper

1. A letter of June 25, 1850 to the architect Baltard insisted on a bed of *"céruse"* (lead carbonate) and boiling oil as a protection against humidity. Actually, Delacroix's anxiety proved justified, for a damage to part of the ceiling from humidity did occur. See *Journal*, April 10, 1860. The wax and oil medium he employed was generally regarded as a means to protect murals from the damage caused by humidity. See, e.g., Jules Varnier, "De la peinture encaustique, apprêts et glutens. Systèmes de Mm. Dussauce, Courtin et Vivet," *L'artiste*, 3rd ser., 3, 1843, 418-19.

2. I believe that the unpublished *Agenda* for 1852 (MS 84, Institut d'Art et d'Archéologie) is by Andrieu. The name "Jenny Le Guilloux" is written on the front cover, but I do not believe the *Agenda* was hers for the following reasons: the name of Delacroix's housekeeper was spelled "Le Guillou," so the misspelling must have been inscribed by someone else; and the author of our *Agenda* was an artist—e.g. he wrote on October 11, 1855 (a separate entry dated in ink): "Je dessine des Poussin"—whereas Jenny was not. It is not Delacroix's, since the handwriting is not his, the many errors in syntax indicate a less educated mind than his, and we already have the *Journal* for 1852. The *Journal* for March 15, 1852 says: "Andrieu worked two days at the beginning of the month; interrupted by the Jury." The fact that Delacroix's assignment to the Jury began on March 6, 1852 fits well with the dates on MS 84. I have found the following specific references to figures in the paintings at Saint-Sulpice: "Mars [1852]: Ange, ombre de sa chair —très sanguine rouge.../Jacob...même tons... draperie blanche...; Mars 5 Vendredi [1852]: homme à cheval, cuirasse...à la peau jaune blanc [sic]...; Mars 6 Samedi: chairs. tons orangés...la demi-teinte au bord de l'ombre est violette/la manche de Jacob et...; Avril 1 Jeudi. Homme à cheval, d'un rouge sale [?]. l'ombre grise. clair violette [?], cheval comme les chamaux [a misspelling of *chameaux*?]...tunique bleu verte, dans l'ombre, ceinture de cuir."

(as on the ornamental frames executed by Boulangé).[3] But since all the pen and pencil sketches are from Delacroix's hand, it is possible to trace the development of his ideas.

A. THE EVOLUTION OF THE SKETCHES

Delacroix relied heavily on sketches for his mural painting. Having worked out his ideas in them, he would outline the composition on the wall in as finished a state as possible, whereupon his helper—at Saint-Sulpice it was mainly Andrieu—would then color in the forms, and the master would retouch with brio and speed wherever needed.[4] Delacroix may have trained Andrieu for this work by having him paint oil sketches, to judge from one made in the early stages of the *Heliodorus* (Fig. 5) and from the color notes for both the *Heliodorus* and the *Jacob* in Andrieu's *Agenda*.[5] After completing the paintings in the chapel, Delacroix wanted to have Andrieu copy them in oil, and possibly the helper painted the two oil sketches in the Prague Museum, one after the *Heliodorus* (Fig. 6), the other after the *Jacob* (Fig. 7) (both 1861 or later and formerly in the George Bernheim Gallery).[6] Delacroix himself, although he had once claimed with romantic fervor to be incapable of copying his own painting, worked earnestly if sporadically to finish a copy of the *St. Michael*.[7] From his approval of the copying of his

3. On the finishing touches see Delacroix's letter of April 28, 1860 to Boulangé. My assumption about the authenticity of the pertinent sketches for the murals is based above all on their uniformly high quality. That many bear the stamp "E.D." of the posthumous sale does not, unfortunately, guarantee that they came from the master's hand. See, e.g., Lee Johnson, "Pierre Andrieu, le cachet E.D. et le chateau de Guermantes," *GBA*, 6th ser., 67, 1966, 99-110, where it is shown that some drawings bearing the stamp "E.D." should be attributed to Andrieu. Henriette Bessis, "Les décorations murales de Pierre Andrieu," *GBA*, 6th ser., 69, 1967, 183-86, does not deny that some drawings falsely bear the stamp "E.D."; but she exculpates Andrieu from Robaut's old accusation of having affixed it to his drawings himself. She believes, rather, that this was probably the act of an unscrupulous dealer who acquired the stamp after Andrieu's death.

4. In September 1850 Delacroix worked closely with Andrieu in this way on the ceiling of the Galerie d'Apollon. See the *Journal* for September 3 and 23, 1850. On the speed of Delacroix's retouches, see René Piot, *Les palettes de Delacroix*, Paris, 1931, 2, where Piot quotes Andrieu's account of clocking the master painting the still life of the *Jacob*, "made at the last moment," which re-

quired "22 minutes and, after 8 days' drying, 16 minutes of retouching."

5. See below for the discussion of the sketch from Fribourg, Switzerland. The *Agenda* of Andrieu is discussed above, in the introduction to this chapter.

6. The Prague Museum dates the two sketches "about 1857" (probably on the basis of Robaut), which I believe mistaken, since both copies are close to the finished murals, including details known to have been painted at the very end, i.e., about 1861: in the *Jacob* the still life, and in the *Heliodorus* the censer, connected with a sketch of March 16, 1861. Delacroix asked Andrieu to copy the *Heliodorus* (in a letter of December 15, 1861), and such a copy already exists, apparently unconnected with the Prague sketches: see the Vente Andrieu, May 6-7, 1892, No. 120.

7. On his inability to copy, see the letter to Planche of May 28, 1831 concerning the *Liberty Leading the People*. On the copy of the *St. Michael*, see the *Journal*, March 27, 1856 and letters to Dutilleux of August 24, 1856, January 30, 1858 (in which he lamented having spoiled the sketch which he had not worked on for a long time), and April 14, 1860 (in which he called the copy "almost finished").

5 Andrieu (?), Sketch of the *Heliodorus*. Fribourg, Switzerland, Musée d'Art et d'Histoire

6 Andrieu (?), Sketch of the *Heliodorus*. Prague Museum, ex-Coll. G. Bernheim (photo: Bulloz)

7 Andrieu (?), Sketch of the *Jacob*. Prague Museum, ex-Coll. G. Bernheim (photo: Witt Library)

murals—he even felt it possible, though difficult, to catch their spirit in black-and-white reproduction—one realizes how essential the compositional idea or "invention" was for Delacroix.[8]

The drawings fall into two main categories: studies of details (the trees for the *Jacob*, the jewels for the *Heliodorus*) and compositional sketches. Many of the studies are so rich in observation that, although one cannot always identify their originals, they seem surely to have been drawn after nature with the intention of providing authentic local color. Delacroix's practice of sketching models for figures in his mural painting can be firmly established for the Library of the Palais Bourbon and for the Hôtel de Ville, and the same thing can be concluded with fair assurance for the decoration at Saint-Sulpice on the basis of his studies of male nudes for the *Heliodorus* in the Besançon Museum.[9] While the artist sketched models chiefly for their movement, he also studied their anatomy, and his interest in certain poses and lighting effects even led him to copy photographs of nudes, which he interpreted not with the tight linearity of an Ingres but in terms of the play of light and dark masses.[10]

In his sketches for the composition, made primarily from imagination, Delacroix transformed the studies from nature in order to fit them into his own framework; hence, it is often hard to connect a study with the painting for which it was made. Not unexpectedly, he advised his pupil De Planet to begin painting his sketches after nature, but to finish them by inspiration, "unconstrained by the model."[11] He often composed, as Géricault did, by a method of tracing

8. In a letter of August 23, 1861 to Charles Blanc, Delacroix wrote: "As to a reproduction, I think that by sending someone in the morning before there are many visitors, one could do something; but it would need a man of some skill, to grasp the spirit of the paintings. During my absence there were attempts to photograph it, which up to now have not succeeded because of the absolute lack of space to move back."

9. Delacroix used models for specific figures in the Library of the Palais Bourbon, some of whose names are known. See the *Correspondance*, letter to De Planet, December 21, 1843. Valuable information is provided by De Planet's *Souvenirs*, 31-32, in which the helper speaks of the use of a model for a figure in one of the pendentives of the Library of the Palais Bourbon: "As this figure is very important and almost nude, above all because the pose could be held, M. Delacroix took a model.... M. Delacroix made a very finished sketch for the muscles, the movement, the shading or the effect. He makes these sketches very quickly, while finishing them as much as he can. The model has to pose for M. Delacroix with the greatest exactness possible. He rests

often, because it is necessary for his [Delacroix's] sketches that the model hold the pose exactly and with sentiment or action." For the Hôtel de Ville, see Delacroix's careful sketch of a shoulder and arm, RF 9544 in the Louvre, Ill. No. 460 in Sérullaz, *Mémorial Delacroix*. A list of female models is inscribed on the first page of the *Journal* for 1859, indicating the artist's continued employment of them at that late date.

10. Delacroix's interest in the movement of the model is attested to by Monet and Bazille, who secretly observed him drawing from a moving model, as Degas and Rodin were to do later. See J. Rewald, *History of Impressionism*, 2nd ed., New York, 1961, 89, where G. Poulain's account in *Bazille et ses amis*, Paris, 1932, 47, is cited. Delacroix's "system of eggs," a technique of building up masses through superimposed oval shapes, seems to have affected his choice of the inner line of mass rather than the outer contour, even though it is not obviously used either in the finished drawings for the murals or in the quick sketches for them. On this system, see De Planet, *Souvenirs*, 33-34.

over an initial quick drawing and then repeating the process, gradually picking out the essential lines, and thus perfecting and purifying his original idea.[12]

Through an arrangement of the sketches for the chapel decorations I have tried to trace the evolution of Delacroix's compositions from the initial gesture-sketches to the final studies for details, in which he clarified and consolidated his ideas. Most of this development occurred rapidly in 1849-1850, with later modifications extending over the decade. Changes in the sketches do not result from haphazard experimentation but from constant refinement and an attempt to resolve basic problems of composition such as the achievement of unity without loss of variety in the poses, gestures and forms. Thus, the complex texture and tangled lines in the more spontaneous early sketches for the *Jacob* are replaced by a controlled simplicity and subtler formal relations; similarly, a gradual elaboration of the architectural ornaments and the accessory objects in the sketches for the *Heliodorus* marks a shift toward greater harmony and decorative richness. To this evolution of the forms there corresponds a change in the mood of the main antagonists of each painting from an early fierceness or anguish to a relative composure.

A chronology of the sketches for Saint-Sulpice can only be tentative and approximate, mainly owing to the scarcity of dated or precisely datable drawings. Most writers date them quite vaguely, and no attempt has even been made to put them into a meaningful sequence.[13] In this

11. See De Planet, *Souvenirs*, 73. For a discussion of Delacroix's technique of drawing as a transformation of nature in contrast to Ingres's approach, see Maurice Denis, "D'Ingres naturaliste à Delacroix poète," *Beaux-Arts*, December 1, 1933, published in Maurice Denis, *Théories*, one of the series "Miroirs de l'art" (Paris, 1964), 131-33.

12. See *Journal*, October 12, 1853; De Planet, *Souvenirs*, 90; and Villot, *Catalogue*, vii. Few of the drawings on tracing paper (*calques*) for the chapel decoration still exist: for the *Heliodorus* there is RF 9515 (see Fig. 45); and for the *St. Michael* there is the sketch in the W. Goetz Collection (Fig. 21) intended for enlargement on the canvas. For Géricault, see Charles Clément, *Géricault: Etudes biographiques et critiques avec le catalogue raisonné d'oeuvres du maître*, Paris, 1867, 102ff., cited by Klaus Berger, *Géricault and His Work*, Lawrence, Kansas, 1955, 50. Possibly the more mature, admired master influenced Delacroix's method of tracing, but this is a speculation.

13. Robaut has confused matters in his catalogue by placing the sketches, which he acknowledged to have been done in 1850, next to the murals in the year 1857. He assigned the murals to this year

because "they really got under way only in 1857," an assertion unsupported in his text and unlikely in the light of Delacroix's ill health during that year, which kept him out of the chapel. See Robaut, *L'oeuvre complet*, 358. Robaut may have been unaware of some of the details of this project; for he even believed that one of the sketches for the *Heliodorus* was by Lassalle-Bordes, who—as will be seen clearly in part two of this chapter—was never engaged for the chapel. On Lassalle-Bordes's sketch, see the annotated copy of Robaut in the Bibliothèque Nationale, No. 1332 bis. For the view, which I believe overgeneralized, that Delacroix's whole stylistic development passed from a romantic youth (1822-31) to a middle period (1832-48) to a classically ordered maturity (1849-63), see Fritz Gysin, *Eugène Delacroix. Studien zu seiner künstlerischen Entwicklung*, Strasbourg, 1929. Raymond Régamey, in *Eugène Delacroix*, 140 and passim, made comments on the artist's development broadly similar to Gysin's (whose book he knew), and, like Gysin, discussed (pp. 113-14) the significance for Delacroix's stylistic evolution of the differences between the 1834 and the 1849 versions of the *Women of Algiers*.

chapter such an arrangement is offered, based mainly on a few dated sketches and on the assumption that the compositional sketches evolve as described above. In some cases stylistic phases can be linked to dated passages in the artist's writings and in archival documents, which establish the following years as critical: 1850, when Delacroix wrote "my compositions are complete"; 1854, 1855, and 1856, when the walls were reprimed; 1856, when there was intensive work in the chapel; and 1861, when important retouches were made.

1. The Sketches for the "St. Michael"

Delacroix's sketches for the *St. Michael* reveal extremely different conceptions, as though the artist had had diffculty resolving certain problems. In order to understand better how Delacroix arrived at his final solution, one has to examine the development of these conceptions.

The sketches for the *St. Michael* can be separated into three groups or versions, corresponding to three phases of their development: Version I, in which St. Michael (distinguished by his central position before the sun) and Lucifer fight at a distance, and in which many figures about equal in size to them swarm among the clouds; Version II, in which the large, fiercely combating figures of St. Michael and Lucifer dominate and in which there are very few figures or clouds in the sky; and Version III, the mural itself, which combines elements from the first two versions, is less effective than the second version and has been criticized for its large empty space, which gives the impression of too little substance stretched over too large an area.

What reasons prompted Delacroix to produce and then to change the first two versions of the theme? I believe that the first version grew directly out of the concurrent project of the Apollo ceiling of the Louvre, which completely dominated Delacroix's thoughts for the period 1849-1851. In *The Triumph of Apollo* the same fundamental scheme as in the first version of the *St. Michael* occurs, of a triumphant figure in the sky (Apollo), surrounded by figures flying in

14. This motif of combat is repeated in the second group at the right, of Minerva and Mercury swooping down upon their demonic enemies. Even the specific postures of certain figures in the sketches for the first version (many of which Delacroix changed in the murals) are very similar to the mural in the Louvre, which probably inspired some of the figures of the *St. Michael:* the female deity above and to the right of Apollo has the same posture as St. Michael, and the figure of Mercury is almost identical with the figures descending from the sky to the left and especially to the right of the archangel, who carries a shield like that of Minerva. In the mural St. Michael gives up the goddess's shield, only to take up her spear.

15. A sketch for the *St. Michael*, RF 9514 (Fig. 20),

contains a marginal note by Delacroix: "The sun dispels the illusions of night and vivifies nature." The text written by the artist for the *Apollo* reads: "...the gods are angry to see the earth abandoned to deformed monsters, impure products of the slime...Minerva, Mercury fall on [the monsters] to exterminate them. Meanwhile they wait for eternal wisdom to repeople the solitude of the universe....Vulcan, god of fire, chases before him the night and the impure vapors....Iris, messenger of the gods, spreads her scarf in the air, symbol of the triumph of light over darkness and over the revolt of the waters." On the probability of a connection with Masonic ideas, see Chapter III, note 72.

16. I suspect that the clearly defined role of the two angels with whips gives them rights of priority

the clouds, with the sun behind him and his conquered enemy writhing on the ground (the distance between victor and vanquished differ greatly in the two works, however).[14] Even the two themes meant similar things to Delacroix, for he viewed both combats as the triumph of light over darkness.[15] Another possible source for Delacroix's use of clouds and figures was Lemoyne's oval ceiling in the Chapel of the Virgin at Saint-Sulpice. It is also likely that Delacroix's work on the other paintings in the chapel affected some figures of the first version: the two flying figures beside St. Michael strongly resemble the two whipping angels in the *Heliodorus*.[16]

In the second version, Delacroix radically changed his composition, as though he were trying to avoid displaying its similarity to that of the *Apollo*;[17] but on the other hand, the obvious resemblance of this new version to the great traditional depictions of the scene as a combat between two large figures (Raphael, Domenichino, Reni) must have displeased him no less. Furthermore, he may have felt that had the proportions of the second version been projected onto the mural, the huge scale of the main figures would have disrupted the harmony between the ceiling and the lower paintings. The final version, that of the mural itself, is an uneasy compromise which registers the incongruity of the two earlier solutions.

The earliest sketch for a ceiling (Fig. 8), in pencil, owned by the Bremen Museum, can be dated approximately to March or April 1849 on the basis of Delacroix's inscription of four themes for the pendentives, Sin, Work, Death and Pain.[18] These are in part linked to the *Journal* entry of April 10, 1849, listing subjects for the ceiling and pendentives of the Chapelle des Fonts Baptismaux, none of which was executed. The composition, which will be considerably altered later, contains the following details: St. Michael raises his right arm high, carries a shield in his left hand and hovers at a distance from the huge Lucifer, whose body, which is in a position the reverse of the mural, seems to spill out of the oval. Another drawing in Bremen (Fig. 9), formerly in the Riesener Collection, probably for Lucifer, shows the sprawling demon

and that the influence therefore went, in this case, from the *Heliodorus* to the *St. Michael*.

17. A figure in sketch RF 29,108 for the Apollo ceiling is not used there. It appears in sketches RF 9514 (Fig. 20) and Robaut 1288 (Fig. 17) for the *St. Michael*, and in the mural itself. It is the figure of a man lying at the lower right, with his head touching the frame, and his up-thrust legs bent at a sharp angle—to the right in the *Apollo* sketch, to the left in the *St. Michael* sketches.

18. This is pointed out in the Museum's catalogue of its Delacroix exhibition, held in 1964, No. 287. Delacroix's inscription reads: *"le Péché*/Adam et Eve/*le travail*/l'hom(m)e labourent/et la fem(m)e devant/...les.../*la mort*/Cain et/Abel/la douleur." On a drawing in the collection of Count Antoine Seilern, London, listed (with ill.) as No. 159, "Studies for 'Le Lever' and an 'Adam and Eve'," in the Delacroix exhibition of 1964 held by the Arts Council of Great Britain, the artist made similar pencil inscriptions: "ou bien elle tient la pomme/la maladie, les maux, le péché les attendent. La mort dans l'arbre de la science...." Mr. Lee Johnson, who wrote the catalogue, dates the Seilern drawing ca. 1847, linking it to the *Journal* entry of May 3, 1847, which concerns "Le Lever" and "Adam and Eve"; but it seems to me that the inscription on No. 159 is sufficiently close to that on the Bremen drawing to warrant dating them together in March or April 1849. No. 160, a drawing showing a more advanced stage of the composition of "Le Lever" than No. 159, and dated 1847/9 by Mr. Johnson, should, I believe, be dated 1849.

8 Delacroix, Sketch for the *St. Michael*. Bremen, Kunsthalle, No. 1928 (photo: Stickelmann)

9 Delacroix, Sketch for the *St. Michael*. Bremen, Kunsthalle (photo: Stickelmann)

with his shield on top of him, quite different from the preceding sketch, except for the unusual left-right reversal of his position. One wonders whether this reversal, which occurs only in this early stage, is connected with the change from a chapel on the north to one on the south side of the church.

Delacroix probably made a number of other sketches gradually working out the positions of the two combatants, but those surviving are already sufficiently like the mural to have been made somewhat later. This first version for the Chapelle des Saints-Anges includes the beautiful oil sketch in the Barnes Foundation, Merion, Pennsylvania (Fig. 10), formerly in the Tatzen-Lund Collection, Copenhagen, and the drawing in the Fogg Art Museum, Cambridge, Mass. (Fig. 11). These sketches for the first version of the *St. Michael*, like those for the two other paintings, were probably completed before October 5, 1850. In this phase Delacroix placed four large figures along the periphery (as in his ceiling at the Hôtel de Ville) in order to link the ceiling to the four pendentive angels; but later he gave up this arrangement, perhaps because it seemed redundant. The angel with a broken sword at the upper left of the Barnes Foundation sketch, who has the same pose as Perseus in the *Perseus and Andromeda* of 1847 (Cone Collection, Baltimore), does not appear in the mural.

A sketch in the Louvre (Fig. 12) studies the figure below Lucifer in more detail than the Fogg drawing. Another sketch (Fig. 13) in the spirit of the Fogg drawing, presents the interlocked fallen bodies beneath Lucifer. The central figure closely resembles the same figure as in the Louvre sketch (Fig. 12). A wash drawing (Fig. 14) is for two fallen demons, one of whom does not appear in any of the other sketches. The other demon with wings is clearly Lucifer, truncated when the page was cut (the stamp ML is misplaced on the page).

Another sketch (Fig. 15) is transitional; for St. Michael still carries a shield as in Version I, and although he and Lucifer are close together and large, as in Version II, the position of their bodies differs from Version II. A study with parts of five figures, which may belong in this period of transition, bears the inscription "22 Août 55."[19]

With Version II belongs a rapidly executed sketch (Fig. 16), which has large central figures and no angels in the clouds. St. Michael stands almost erect, both hands gripping the spear. A pencil sketch from a private collection, bearing the stamp of the Darcy Collection, No. 521 in the *Mémorial Delacroix* of 1963, shows a wingless Lucifer over whom hovers St. Michael, aiming his spear at Lucifer's chest. The St. Michael of this sketch and the sketch above (Fig. 16) re-

19. I have not seen this study. It is mentioned in Robaut, *L'oeuvre complet*, 344, No. 1285 bis, one of the handwritten marginalia of the Bibliothèque Nationale copy, which reads: "Etude pour le plafond de l'Eglise Saint-Sulpice—croquis de fragments de cinq figures. Dessin mine de plomb: 22 x 34½ daté en haut à dr.: '22 Août '55'. Appt. à M. Alexis Vollon."

10 Delacroix, Oil study for the *St. Michael*. Merion, Pa., The Barnes Foundation (© 1966 by The Barnes Foundation)

11 Delacroix, Pencil sketch for the *St. Michael*. Cambridge, Mass., The Fogg Art Museum, No. 19342

12 Delacroix, Sketch for the *St. Michael*. Paris, Louvre, RF 9986

13 Delacroix, Sketch for the *St. Michael*. Paris, Louvre, RF 9985

14 Delacroix, Sketch for the *St. Michael*. Paris, Louvre, RF 10,008

15 Delacroix, Sketch for the *St. Michael*. Paris, Louvre, RF 9535

16 Delacroix, Sketch for the *St. Michael*. Paris, Louvre, RF 24,214

semble one another in their wings (the left pointing down, the right on a horizontal) and legs (the left lower than the right). Robaut No. 1288 (Fig. 17) contains fewer figures than the Louvre sketch (Fig. 16) so that the confrontation of St. Michael and Lucifer stands out clearly. Flames rise at the left and smoke mingles with the clouds, partially covering some figures strewn on the ground. A demon on his back, at the right side, closely resembles a demon located similarly in the mural. The figure beneath Lucifer reverses the position of an earlier sketch (Fig. 12) and of its counterpart in the mural. The swarms of angels flying in the air and heaped on the ground of Version I have been replaced by several broken forms on the ground and by a monstrous Lucifer shrieking defiance at his tormentor. In the two sketches of Lucifer (Fig. 18) where he closely resembles his counterpart in the Robaut sketch (Fig. 17), one senses the quivering rage of the demon.

The sketch from the Musée Bonnat, Bayonne (Fig. 19), concentrates on the large central pair of St. Michael and Lucifer and is quite similar to the Robaut (Fig. 17). The secondary figures differ much more from the mural than do the two main figures, and the demon beneath Lucifer does not appear in the final version.

It was perhaps this second version which Delacroix actually placed on the ceiling in 1855-1856, but which was probably destroyed when the wall was scraped and reprimed in September 1856.[20] Two sketches for the second version suggest this possibility (Figs. 20 and 21). The first (Fig. 20), with its notes, guidelines and large size (15⅖" x 20⅖"), seems to have been intended for execution on the ceiling. The heroic figures of St. Michael and Lucifer completely dominate the space. A sketch in pencil and black chalk from the Walter Goetz Collection (Fig. 21) presents the large form of Lucifer with a demon just below him.[21] The drawing mat contains a grid and is inscribed with numerals, implying a similar intention to enlarge it.

Delacroix probably made drawings for the *St. Michael*, and certainly made an oil copy of it after 1856 (which I have not seen) before working out his final composition.[22] In September 1858 the painting was glued to the ceiling, finished except for retouches.[23]

2. The Sketches for the "Jacob"

A sketch in the Cabinet des Dessins at the Louvre (Fig. 22) contains what seems to be the earliest sketch for the *Jacob*. It is quickly drawn, and one cannot tell whether there are two separate figures in the foreground or two trial positions of the interlocked wrestlers. The com-

20. For details, see the discussion in the next part of this chapter.
21. This drawing, formerly in the P. Dubaut Collection, was once owned by Degas.
22. This copy was ordered by Legentil of Arras through Delacroix's acquaintance, the painter Constant Dutilleux. See the *Journal*, March 27, 1856, and letter to Dutilleux, March 5, 1857. The only oil sketch for the ceiling I know, that of the Barnes Foundation, belongs in the first version and so seems too early to be the one for Dutilleux.

23. See the *Journal*, September 5, 1858.

17 Delacroix, Sketch for the *St. Michael*. Whereabouts unknown. Robaut 1288 (photo: Witt Library)

18 Delacroix, Sketch for the *St. Michael*. Paris, Louvre, RF 9596

19 Delacroix, Sketch for the *St. Michael*. Bayonne, France, Musée Bonnat (photo: Witt Library)

20 Delacroix, Sketch for the *St. Michael.* Paris, Louvre, RF 9514

21 Delacroix, Sketch (pencil on tracing paper) for the *St. Michael*. Paris, Coll. Walter Goetz (photo: courtesy of Mr. Goetz)

le cavalier sambride

22 Delacroix, Sketch for the *Jacob*. Paris, Louvre, RF 24,215

position is divided into the large figures below and the branches or clouds above. Later Delacroix will link these two sections by means of tree trunks running from the ground to the arch above. The small figure-like form above the wrestlers may be intended for one of the figures in the caravan.

In 1849-1850 Delacroix made a number of studies of an oak tree, mainly of "le chêne Prieur," but also of "le chêne d'Antin," both in the forest of Sénart at Champrosay, near Paris, where the artist owned a house. While these sketches were probably made with the *Jacob* in mind, they bear less upon the details of the trees in the mural than upon their energetic spirit.[24]

A sketch of "le chêne Prieur" (Fig. 23) is dated 1849 and so probably was drawn in November 1849, when Delacroix was at Champrosay. The imprecise dating (cf. Fig. 27, below) suggests that the sketch was classified long after it was drawn, during one of the artist's periodic attempts to arrange his vast production. Several details connect it with the *Jacob*: the arched top, the central placement of the trunk, with its branches extending along the arch, and the vertically oriented mass of foliage at the right, destined to be rotated clockwise in the mural. All the tree sketches indicate the trunk's rough bark, and several (see Figs. 23-26 and 28) have a brisk and vigorous stroke reminiscent of Van Gogh. The single big tree will be split into three contiguous trees in the mural. A railing no longer encloses the tree, as in the sketch.

One sketch (Fig. 24) is a study of the upper part of the same tree, with its characteristic inclination, textured bark, and contour of the left side. The note, "mousse éclairée au bord," and the two lines pointing precisely to the branches where the moss appears, indicate Delacroix's interest in carefully observed details. Another study (Fig. 25) presents the same tree, but from the opposite side, while a study (Fig. 26) of a different tree (perhaps the "chêne d'Antin") shows the tree trunk as a dominant form from which subsidiary branches emerge.

One of the sketches (Fig. 27) bears the words "13 ou 14 mai," with unclear characters below, cut in half by the lower edge of the drawing, probably reading "50."[25] The implied edge of the foliage and of the hatching is arch-shaped, very much like the top of the mural; but, far from

24. Delacroix was interested in the landscape at Champrosay before and after composing the *Jacob*. The great sale of his work at the Hôtel Drouot in 1864 alone lists under No. 603, "Etudes de paysages, arbres, etc. faites à Champrosay de 1848 à 1863. 46 feuilles." Number 664 bis of this sale (according to Robaut's Catalogue No. 1834) included 18 notebooks with many studies made in the same forest over several years. It would be of considerable interest to connect these and other undated landscapes with dated works, and on the basis of the resulting chronological ordering, to study the evolution of Delacroix's approach to landscape. In the months immediately

preceding his definitive commission at Saint-Sulpice, Delacroix became very interested in flower and landscape motifs, which he observed in his walks through the woods at Champrosay. For his touching and poetic description of this countryside, see the *Journal*, October 7 and 13, 1849. An entry of August 19, 1854 compared his struggles in life to those of trees growing in barren soil, whose branches are "twisted and knotty."

25. Delacroix was often only approximately correct in his dating of his sketches; perhaps in this case he waited until after he returned to Paris to arrange and date them. It is also possible that the

23 Delacroix, Sketch for the *Jacob*. Paris, Louvre, RF 9428

24 Delacroix, Sketch for the *Jacob*. Paris, Louvre, RF 9429

25 Delacroix, Sketch for the *Jacob*. Paris, Louvre, RF 9430

26 Delacroix, Sketch for the *Jacob*. Paris, Louvre, RF 9433

27 Delacroix, Sketch for the *Jacob*. Paris, Louvre, RF 9427

transplanting the whole tree into the painting, Delacroix seems to have distributed features of it among the trees at the right (the contour of the root, the bent form of the branch), in the center (the long lowermost branch to the left of the tree) and at the left of the composition (its largest bifurcation and its inclination).

Another sketch (Fig. 28) is inscribed "17 mai" and slightly lower, inverted, "J'étais Jupiter assistant au combat de cet Achille et de cet Hector." This clearly repeats a *Journal* entry of May 17, 1850, which describes in Aesopian terms a fight between insects won "with distributive justice" by what he thought the weaker: "I saw the combat of a spider and a wasp.... I was the Jupiter contemplating the fight of this Achilles and this Hector...."[26] The tree, probably "le chêne Prieur," contains the same essential profile of a projecting sawn limb and bump below on one side as in Figs. 23-25, 28, and 42, but faces in the opposite direction. Its form is not essentially changed by the addition of twigs, e.g. to the sawn limb.

Delacroix made several sketches during 1849-1850 of the two wrestling figures separately and within the whole composition.

The Albertina sketches[27] were probably drawn on the same day early in April, 1850, for they are similar in technique (pencil on paper), line quality and details of the figures. One (Fig. 29) presents the composition in a form which is much closer than the earlier Louvre sketch (Fig. 22) to the finished version: the wrestlers are at the left, the caravan at the right, a still life appears below to the right of the wrestlers, and a tree in the center reaches up to the top of the frame. But aside from the sketchiness (e.g. it is unclear whether there are two thick branches of one tree or two separate trees), there are differences from the mural: we find a bush to the right of Jacob, instead of the hill with an arabesque contour, and the angel's left arm is raised with the elbow up instead of down, a position retained in the other Albertina sketches.

A page of three gesture-sketches (Fig. 30) presents the wrestlers in a reversed position. Delacroix has here engaged in a series of trial positions using almost nude figures (the angel's cloak and Jacob's robe are suggested) and an angel without wings.

One Albertina sketch (Fig. 31) is inscribed "acecinctus"(?),[28] which I believe to be a misspelling of "accinctus," a word entered in the *Journal* on April 10, 1850 after a visit from the former consul general at Tangiers: "He tells me that among the Romans one called *accincti* the soldiers and *incincti* the citizens. It is as in Morocco...." The artist probably inscribed the word on our sketch soon after this conversation in order not to forget it, and also perhaps because he had just

drawing was among the works inventoried by the artist in April 1857 before he moved to a new studio. See Delacroix, *Journal*, III, 89, Joubin's n. 1 for April 1, 1857.

26. Delacroix's word *mouche* is usually translated "fly," which does not fit his description. *Mouche* is used loosely in French to include the wasp, although the artist, no entomologist, may in fact have mistakenly intended to mean "fly."

27. In the Graphische Sammlung, Albertina, Vienna, whose numbers I have used.

28. The Bremen Museum, in its catalogue of the Delacroix exhibition held there in 1964, No. 314, offers the reading "aminctus," which it does not explain or support. Professor Schapiro originally proposed to me the present reading, but not until it could be connected with the *Journal* entry could it become secure.

28 Delacroix, Sketch for the *Jacob*. Paris, Louvre, RF 9431

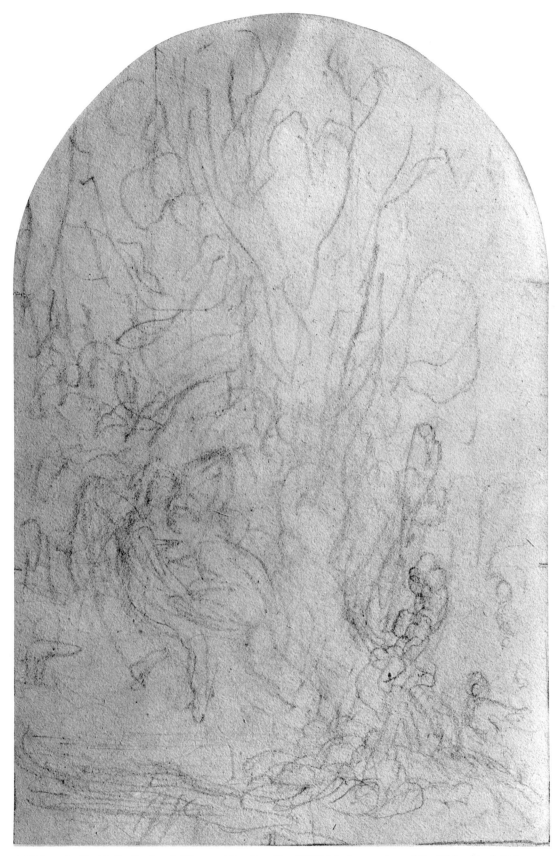

29 Delacroix, Sketch for the *Jacob*. Vienna, Albertina, No. 45,875 (photo: courtesy of the Bildarchiv d. Ost. Nationalbibliothek)

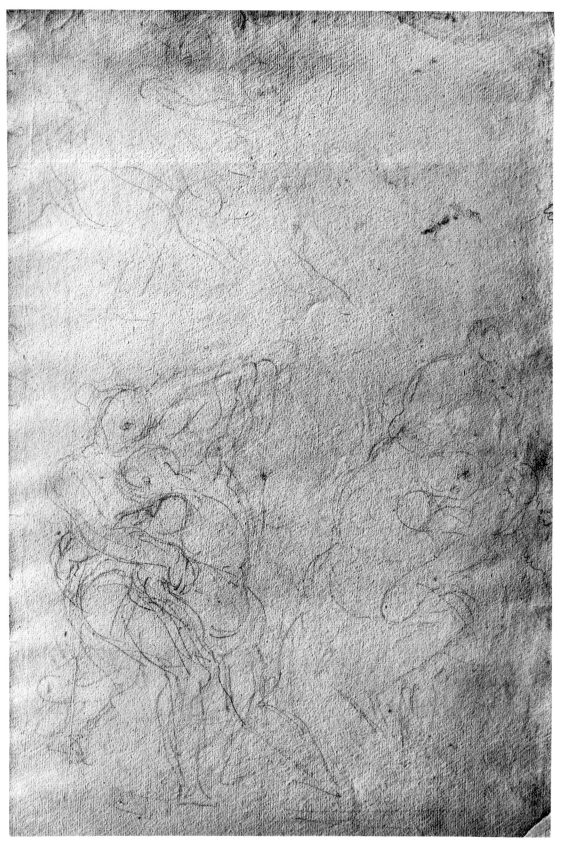

30 Delacroix, Sketch for the *Jacob*. Vienna, Albertina, No. 45,874 (photo: courtesy of the Bildarchiv d. Ost. Nationalbibliothek)

31 Delacroix, Sketch for the *Jacob*. Vienna, Albertina, No. 24,515 (photo: courtesy of the Bildarchiv d. Ost. Nationalbibliothek)

made the decision to give Jacob arms like the *accincti*, rather than a simple girdle like the *incincti*; for apparently no drawing prior to the Fogg sketch, to be discussed shortly, clearly contains weapons (one [Fig. 29] seems to have only clothing). The inscription also provides another instance of the artist's comparing Rome to Morocco.

Another of the group from the Albertina (Fig. 32) resembles the preceding sketch (Fig. 31) in some details (such as in the three spade-shaped bunches of the angel's hair), but is more firmly drawn and has fewer trial lines.

A spirited pencil drawing in the Bremen Museum, formerly in the Riesener Collection (Fig. 33), was executed quickly and with few details, like the Albertina sketches. The overpowering size of the angel, the separation of the figures, who wrestle at arm's length, and the upright posture of Jacob are peculiar to this sketch.

A sketch at the Musée de Peinture et de Sculpture, Grenoble (Fig. 34), places masks of bestiality on the wrestlers' faces, perhaps influenced by concurrent work on the Lucifer of the *St. Michael*. The impulse which prompted Delacroix to characterize the wrestlers in this demonic way is difficult to determine, and in his later sketches he retreated from the horrible combination of athletic form and bestial face. We can only admire the powerful expressiveness of this image and wonder at its personal meaning to the artist.

A sketch of the wrestlers from the Roger-Marx Collection (Fig. 35)[29] seems to belong in the same period as the Albertina sketches, and like one of the Albertina sketches (Fig. 30), it reverses the position of the two figures, while the angel's hair recalls the spade-shaped bunches of hair of the angel in other sketches (Figs. 31 and 32). The clasped hands are away from the spectator in order not to block the view of the wrestlers. The shadows on the ground go in the same direction as those in the mural. The angel's back is to the sun, and his face is in shadow, seen frontally, whereas in the mural his face is lighted by the sun and in profile.

A sketch in the Fogg Art Museum (Fig. 36), inscribed "vert" at the left, resembles the preceding sketch, not only in similarly reversing the main figures, but in such details as the facial expressions, the clasped hands and forearm, and the swirl of Jacob's robe, which is parted in two. Certain differences from the preceding sketch place it closer to the finished version: the angel's right wing curves in an arabesque similar to that of its counterpart in the mural, the angel's hair is less obviously disheveled and the caravan figures are here indicated clearly for the first time. There are differences from the mural: the whole composition is reversed; a sword

29. Displayed as No. 182 in the 1963 exhibition at the *atelier* of Delacroix; No. 184 in that exhibit, in ink, ca. 9" x 6" and from a "private collection," is almost identical with No. 182.

32 Delacroix, Sketch for the *Jacob*. Vienna, Albertina, No. 44,547 (photo: courtesy of the Bildarchiv d. Ost. Nationalbibliothek)

33 Delacroix, Sketch for the *Jacob*. Bremen, Kunsthalle

34 Delacroix, Sketch for the *Jacob*. Grenoble, Musée de Peinture et de Sculpture

35 Delacroix, Sketch for the *Jacob*. Paris, Coll. C. Roger-Marx

36 Delacroix, Sketch for the *Jacob*. Cambridge, Mass., The Fogg Art Museum, No. 1934.3

between Jacob's legs and a spear are added in the mural, and three majestic trees will replace in the mural the five trees which seem dwarfed or like one large hedge.

A second sketch from the Roger-Marx Collection (Fig. 37) is similar to the Fogg Art Museum sketch in several details, except that the wrestlers are not in a reversed position. As in the two preceding sketches, the angel's expression is less troubled and begins to approach that of the calmer finished version. The angel's coiffure is likewise less disheveled, less "troubled." The steep slope of the figures, with the angel much above Jacob, is unusual and resulted from the paper's being cut catty-cornered, probably by the estate, whose stamp "E.D." is aligned with the cut edge and not with the light ground-line on the sketch.

Up to this point, all of the sketches for the *Jacob* seem to belong in the period ending October 5, 1850, on which date Delacroix wrote, referring to the three paintings: "My compositions are complete." I know of no sketches between 1850 and 1854. Possibly there are some which I have not seen for the period just before and just after April 24, 1854, when the walls were reprimed and Delacroix again set to work on the murals.

A sketch in the Morgan Library (ex-Germain Seligman Collection) was probably made in 1856 (Fig. 38). Robaut linked it to a sketch dated 1856 and assigned it to the same year.[30] In it, Delacroix made a decisive change in the composition by reducing the tree forms to three large trees, two of which intertwine. The artist did important work on the *Jacob* in 1856, and on March 13, 1856 he noted that he wanted Boulangé to sketch in the landscape background. At this stage in particular we are aware of the correspondence between the interlocking wrestlers and the twisting trees and between their contours and those of the hills around them. Rough-barked trees screen off the foreground, but openings allow the distant background to show through. This sketch differs from the mural in the following: the crowns of the trees are still not dense, and many spots of light break through; the space in which the caravan moves has still a nearly vertical contour, whereas in the mural this contour is prolonged and tapered leftward; the area below the wrestlers is filled with scribbles suggesting grass instead of the still life; and Jacob's robe still flies high behind his right arm.

A third sketch from the C. Roger-Marx Collection (Fig. 39) is closely related to the one from the Morgan Library, especially in the "mountain contours" of the angel's wings, but also in details of the anatomy and dress, and in the indication of the still life beside Jacob's right leg. Perhaps this sketch was drawn just before Delacroix began the Morgan Library drawing of the

30. See the Annotated Robaut at the Bibliothèque Nationale, No. 1328 bis.

37 Delacroix, Sketch for the *Jacob*. Paris, Coll. C. Roger-Marx

38 Delacroix, Sketch for the *Jacob*. New York, Pierpont Morgan Library

39 Delacroix, Sketch for the *Jacob*. Paris, Coll. C. Roger-Marx

whole composition. If so, it would constitute a transition between the earlier Roger-Marx sketches and the Morgan Library sketch.

The oil sketch on paper mounted on canvas owned by E. V. Thaw and Co. (Fig. 40) combines the figures of the last sketch with the composition and landscape of the one from the Morgan Library. Delacroix seems first to have made pencil outlines which he then colored in oil, finally adding brush and pen lines to clarify or strengthen his effects. This process has resulted in a work which, while richly colored, looks curiously like an exercise, with overemphatic lines and highlights. It may have been a preparation for the Vienna sketch painted wholly in brush and oil.

The Vienna oil sketch (Fig. 41), like both the preceding oil sketch and the Morgan Library drawing, shows clearly the parallel between the struggling figures and the intertwining trees above them (the tree at the far left resembles a person with arms flung up excitedly). This sketch may have been done later than either of the aforementioned studies, perhaps in 1856, if it is linked to Delacroix's note of August 26, 1856, stating that he had worked again on a "group" in the *Jacob*. The relative calm of his wrestling athletes at once brings to mind certain studies of nudes for the *Heliodorus*, probably drawn in August 1856.[31] Delacroix painted at least one more sketch after this (which I have not seen), *viz.*, one described by Robaut as bearing a date and which he placed in 1856.[32]

During 1857 Delacroix continued to sketch oak trees, e.g. on his trip to Plombières; but at this point they probably influenced his composition only slightly (see Figs. 43 and 44).[33]

In a sketch at the Louvre (Fig. 42) inscribed "13 mai mercredi," and so apparently sketched in 1857 at Champrosay, the twisting branch at the right is (as in the Morgan Library sketch) much in the spirit of the branches on the right side of the mural.[34] But with the Vienna sketch, despite obvious differences from the mural, such as the substitution of the lion's skin for the simple white cloak here worn by Jacob and the change in position and contents of the still life, we already approach the final phase, when the strained, tortuous quality in the landscape and in the wrestlers is smoothed away.

3. The Sketches for the "Heliodorus"

A quick gesture-drawing (Fig. 22—discussed above in connection with the *Jacob*), which seems to be the first of the earliest series of sketches made late in 1849 or early in 1850, juxtaposes

31. See the discussion of the Besançon drawing below, in part 3 of this section.

32. The annotations to Robaut 1328 bis (referred to above) are: "Avant 1328. Lutte de Jacob et de l'Ange. Toile. 56 x 40 daté au bas à gauche...."

33. André Lefèvre, in "Delacroix et les Vosges," *Le pays Lorrain*, 36, 1955, 145, argues that an oak tree, "le chêne de l'impératrice," which the artist saw on his trip to Plombières in 1857 influenced the *Jacob*; but his evidence is not convincing.

34. Sérullaz, *Mémorial Delacroix*, No. 518, first noted that only the year 1857 is consistent with the information inscribed on the sketch and the fact that it was drawn at Champrosay.

40 Delacroix, Sketch for the *Jacob*. New York, E. V. Thaw and Co. (photo: courtesy of Mr. E. V. Thaw)

41 Delacroix, Sketch for the *Jacob*, oil. Vienna, Kunsthistorisches Museum

42 Delacroix, Sketch for the *Jacob*. Paris, Louvre, RF 9432

43 The "chêne d'Antin," in the forest of Sénart, France, two views (Jack Spector)

44 The "chêne Prieur," in the forest of Sénart, France, two views (Jack Spector)

projects for the two lower paintings. The drawing for the *Heliodorus* indicates the bare essentials of its composition: the horse and the angel at the right that fall on the cringing Heliodorus, the dais and the great central column and the group about Onias on the balcony. There are many differences from the mural, notably the round arch at the right, which is changed to a flat lintel in the mural, and the absence of important things like the horse's bridle (there is a note by Delacroix, "le cavalier sans bride"), the central drape and the stairway with the running girl. In his half-sitting position, Delacroix's Heliodorus (unlike the mural) resembles Raphael's Heliodorus.

In a particularly energetic sketch (Fig. 45) Delacroix tried out several positions for the rider's spear and for the right angel's whip. The angel rider shows obvious differences from later sketches and the final version: he lacks wings and holds a spear rather than a baton. Heliodorus no longer half-sits but is stretched out beneath the punishing angels.

Another sketch from the Louvre (Fig. 46) is more detailed and more crowded. Now Heliodorus lies on a dais with a helmet beside his head, and there is a soldier in the right foreground. In the angles of their bodies and in their postures, the main figures (the angels, Heliodorus) approximate the final solution more closely; but the composition is much less clear than in the mural. The concentration of forms is confusing; e.g. Heliodorus' left leg fuses with the left leg of the horse, and the angel's face is covered by Heliodorus' right hand. The soldier behind the dais at the right of Heliodorus makes his appearance here for the first time. His form will undergo various changes before the finished version, such as in the bent position of his right arm, which is too symmetrical with that of the whipping angel facing him. The rider differs markedly from the final form: his wings are tentatively drawn, and his helmet is simpler. He now carries a shorter spear, suggesting the later baton.

A drawing from the Huet Collection (Fig. 47) concentrates on the ferocious attack of the angel on Heliodorus. There are two trial positions of the right angel's legs. The still life, very detailed in this figure study, is linked to the group of figures by the repetition of the curved line of the vases in the horse's leg and tail, the angel's sash and the rider's helmet.

A sketch from the Musée Condé, Chantilly (Fig. 48), is the earliest full-scale drawing showing architecture close in form (but not in decoration) to the finished version. Much livelier than the earlier version (cf. Fig. 22), this sketch has the big drape added, with its powerful thrust downward, and numerous figures gesticulating in the background. The horse, still without a

45 Delacroix, Sketch for the *Heliodorus*. Paris, Louvre, RF 9515

46 Delacroix, Sketch for the *Heliodorus*. Paris, Louvre, RF 23,322

47 Delacroix, Sketch for the *Heliodorus*. Ex-Coll. P. Huet, present whereabouts unknown

48 Delacroix, Sketch for the *Heliodorus*. Chantilly, Musée Condé (photo: Archives photographiques)

bridle, tosses his mane about wildly. There is much more crowding of the forms as compared with the final painting; for the angels are proportionally larger and press closer to one another. Heliodorus still thrusts his left hand over the top step of the dais (whereas in the finished version his arm does not even reach the edge of the dais), and the rider's wing and the tip of the right angel's cloak reach up to the top step (whereas in the finished version they are considerably below it). Because in the mural Delacroix did not enlarge his figures or the areas above the balcony in the same proportions as the frame, he increased the space between the rider's wing and the balcony. The bearded soldier in the foreground who here presses himself toward the Heliodorus group becomes more restrained in the finished version and casts his look down.

A sketch in the Fogg Art Museum for the *Heliodorus* (Fig. 49) is very close to the Chantilly sketch, but seems slightly later. I believe that it can be connected with the two other sketches in the Fogg Art Museum, one for *St. Michael* and one for *Jacob*, which I have already discussed and which belong stylistically among the earlier versions. The sketches for the *Heliodorus* and for the *Jacob* are strikingly similar in technique: over a lightly scribbled drawing, emphasizing value rather than line, Delacroix picked out here and there with a swift incisive touch the main contours. The sizes of the *Heliodorus* (22⅞" x 15½") and of the *Jacob* (22¼" x 15⅛") are almost identical, and the sheets for both sketches are similarly composed of smaller sheets pasted together. In its technique and size, the sketch for the *St. Michael* (11¼" x 14") sufficiently resembles the other two sketches to warrant connecting all three. The concurrent execution of large-sized drawings for each of the murals strongly suggests that they were the sketches to which Delacroix referred in his *Journal* entry of February 27, 1850: "I am working on the sketches *(croquis)* to submit to the Prefecture," and which his collaborator Lassalle-Bordes saw during March 1850.[35] The sketch for the *Heliodorus* bears the inscription "Voir Jean Duvet pour les Anges." Delacroix knew and studied the work of this vigorous and fantastic sixteenth century French engraver, probably at the Cabinet des Estampes, B. N.;[36] however, I have found no models in Duvet's work for any of the figures in the *Heliodorus*.[37] The reference to Duvet primarily registers Delacroix's interest at this stage of his work in the older artist's intense and violent style. The important, but temporary, insertion of a soldier between Heliodorus and the

35. In MS 245, Institut d'Art et d'Archéologie, Paris, the letter written much later to Burty and dating June 20, 1879 contains the following statement by Lassalle-Bordes: "A mon retour à Paris, en Mars 1850...il me montra les esquisses des peintures et ce que je devais faire à Saint-Sulpice arrêtées définitivement." For further discussion see below, this chapter.

36. It is known that Delacroix was a friend of Atoch, an employee of the Bibliothèque Nationale, up to 1831. See e.g. Delacroix, *Correspondance*, I, 267, note of A. Joubin. M. Adhémar of the Cabi-

net des Estampes, B.N., has kindly offered the opinion that Delacroix probably did work at the Cabinet des Estampes during the thirties and forties at least. The artist inscribed with Duvet's name a sketch (RF 9300) for the Palais Bourbon, dating after 1833. Part of Duvet's *Apocalypse* engravings of 1571 were among the possessions of the Cabinet des Estampes when the artist worked there.

37. The Baltimore Museum (supported by F. S. Grubar, "Two Drawings by Delacroix," *Baltimore Museum of Art News*, 17[1-6], October 1953)

49 Delacroix, Sketch for the *Heliodorus*. Cambridge, Mass., The Fogg Art Museum, No. 1934.4

foreground soldier serves to link them. This soldier disappears in later sketches but reappears in the mural in a very different position and attitude.

A group of Louvre sketches (Figs. 50-58) are for the decoration of the temple walls and columns. These sketches probably date in March or April, 1850; for they seem to be associated with Jules Laurens's illustrations for a book on Persian architecture, which Delacroix saw on March 11, 1850.[38] After establishing the final form of the architecture in the Fogg and Chantilly sketches, he studied the question of its decoration. Significantly, Delacroix designed the architecture and the decoration separately, and had no single model from which to derive his temple complete. The lions' heads (Fig. 50) are for the frieze decorating the walls between the columns. The artist tentatively sketched the decoration of the lower doors, of the central columns and of the beams of the upper doors (Fig. 55), to which his inscription refers: "Au milieu de la poutre [beam] de chaque côté." Most of these forms will be changed in the mural; in particular, the complicated pairing of the snakes with their tails entwined will be simplified to a rectangle with a central disc.

Another sketch (Fig. 56) develops the above motifs, especially the snake on the corbel of the lower door, vaguely indicated earlier. The firmly drawn and complicated profiles need not suggest only the Orient, inasmuch as such forms are found also in classic and Renaissance art.[39] For the corbel Delacroix made a series of four renderings, three in perspective; going from left to right, we can study the steps whereby he progressively adapted its contour to the snake decorating it. The drawings in the top half of the sheet represent advanced stages in the development

lists a drawing from its Lucas Collection bearing a similar inscription, "les anges de Jean Duvet," as a study for the *Heliodorus*, to which it seems linked in the following ways: there is a figure at the left seated in a posture not unlike a cavalier's; horizontal figures resemble the whipping angel on the left of Heliodorus; and a figure at the top holding a weapon in his right hand and wearing mail over his chest is very much in the spirit of the angel rider, especially in sketches such as RF 9515 (Fig. 45). But the aforementioned weapon is a sword, which appears in no sketch for the *Heliodorus*, and indeed has nothing to do with the story. Furthermore, the Museum's sketch can be linked securely to two projects for the ceiling of the Palais Bourbon of 1833-38, *Justice* and *War*. The inscription "Jean Duvet" appears on one of the sketches for the *Justice*, RF 9300; the figure in mail with the sword very closely resembles the central figure in *War*, Robaut 533; and other resemblances can be found to the poses

of figures in RF 9970, a sketch for *Justice*. The complicated borrowings of Delacroix from his own earlier work and from the work of others, and the subsequent transformations of those borrowings, explain the presumed connection of the sketch in the Baltimore Museum with the *Heliodorus*. Mr. Douglas H. Gordon of Baltimore owns a fine drawing sometimes mistakenly associated with the angel rider of the *Heliodorus*, but which is probably for a mounted hunter.

38. Laurens's illustrations appeared later in Hommaire de Hell's *Voyage en Turquie et Perse*, published in 1853. See the next chapter for further discussion of Laurens's studies.

39. This is in keeping with the exotic decorative details in Laurens's drawings of Persian architecture; for, as Delacroix noted in his *Journal* on March 11, 1850, the Persian "capitals, frieze and cornice" which he studied in Laurens's drawings were "entirely in the Greek proportions, but with ornaments which completely renew it...."

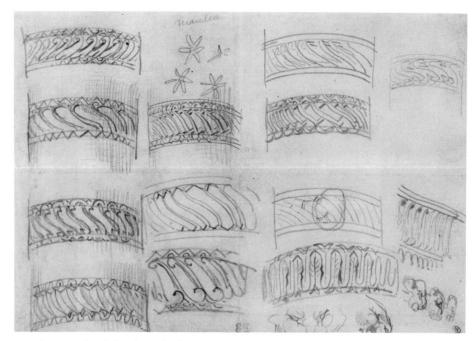

50 Delacroix, Sketch for the *Heliodorus*. Paris, Louvre, RF 9519

51 Delacroix, Sketch for the *Heliodorus*. Paris, Louvre, RF 9520r

52 Delacroix, Sketch for the *Heliodorus*. Paris, Louvre, RF 9520v

53 Delacroix, Sketch for the *Heliodorus*. Paris, Louvre, RF 9536

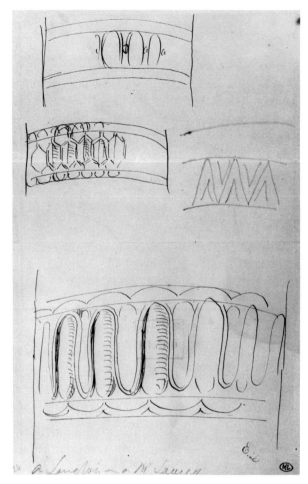

54 Delacroix, Sketch for the *Heliodorus*. Paris, Louvre, RF 9540

55 Delacroix, Sketch for the *Heliodorus*. Paris, Louvre, RF 9518

56 Delacroix, Sketch for the *Heliodorus*. Paris, Louvre, RF 9521

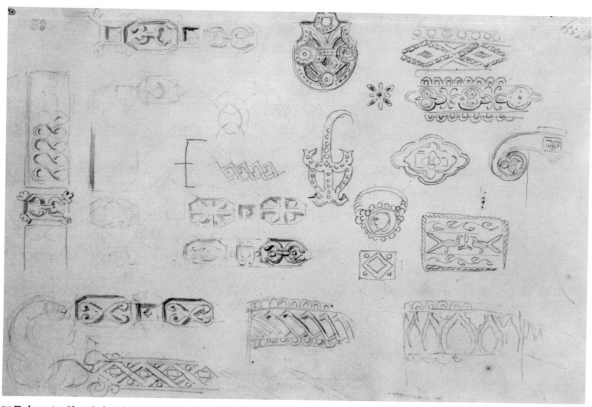

57 Delacroix, Sketch for the *Heliodorus*. Paris, Louvre, RF 9522

of the stepped form of the upper doorways and of the decorative frieze over the lintel, which is simplified from the entwined snakes of the earlier sketch (Fig. 55).

One page devoted to studies of jewelry (Fig. 57) from different periods and places as sources for decorative motifs[40] was probably made in 1850 at the Louvre, where Delacroix could examine rich collections of precious objects while painting the *Triumph of Apollo*.[41] It is noteworthy that, whereas the jewelry in the bottom row corresponds to objects in other sketches for the *Heliodorus*, the buckles, bracelets and rings in the top row have no clear connection with the murals. This suggests that Delacroix drew from real models above and then applied his discoveries of new forms to the *Heliodorus* designs below. Here, as in the previous sketch, he introduced new forms and then reworked and adapted them to the needs of his composition.

A sketch (Fig. 58) rendered throughout in a graphic shorthand, contains what may be the latest in the series of studies for the temple decoration, together with a gesture-sketch which concentrates on the punishment of Heliodorus. This fascinating sheet reveals the artist's continuing search for motifs and juxtaposes studies of jewelry and designs derived from them which tentatively decorate the architecture. Here Delacroix, exploring at once figures in motion and objects at rest, combines the two categories of his earlier studies.

After this initial cluster of drawings, there are no others for the *Heliodorus* before 1856; but two quite similar oil sketches for the painting—one from the Museum of Le Havre (Fig. 59) and another from the Museum of Art and History in Fribourg, Switzerland (see Fig. 5)—indicate the state of his composition before that date. Andrieu may have painted the sketch from Fribourg (No. 86 in the posthumous sale of Delacroix in 1864); whereas the sketch from Le Havre, which is freer and less detailed, and which was also in Delacroix's possession on his death (No. 52 of the posthumous sale of 1864), was most likely painted by the master.[42] The sketch, presumably by Andrieu, which was based on drawings such as the one from the Huet Collection or the one at Chantilly (or possibly on a lost oil sketch by Delacroix) should be dated 1852, since the helper's *Agenda* for March and April of that year contains some precious color notes for the paintings in the chapel, probably in connection with just such sketches.[43] In both sketches a striking new feature is introduced, which is not found in earlier drawings but is found in the mural: the horse now has a bridle.

40. Delacroix throughout his career made studies of coins, jewelry, armor, etc. from museums and private collections. The two auction marks and the Louvre stamp are placed upside down on the page.

41. The Gallery of Apollo, whose ceiling Delacroix was concurrently decorating, held then, as now, cases filled with jewelry. See the *Journal*, March 21, 1850, among other references to the project.

42. This is the opinion of Sérullaz, *Mémorial Delacroix*, No. 509, and of Lee Johnson, *BurlM*, 105, 1963, 301. The artist's weakness is evident, for example, in the left angel, whose arm, leg and whip seem, with the horse's leg, to emerge like spokes from the hub of his right hand, resulting in a confusion of spatial relations.

43. For Andrieu's *Agenda* of 1852, see the introduction to this chapter. The sketch certainly cannot date earlier than October 1851, when Andrieu was first mentioned by Delacroix for the chapel.

58 Delacroix, Sketch for the *Heliodorus*. Paris, Louvre, RF 9517

59 Delacroix, Sketch for the *Heliodorus*. Le Havre, Musée, No. 82

The Besançon Museum has three studies (Figs. 60-62), similar in style and technique, of male nudes, one for the angel rider, and one for each of the two whipping angels, which can perhaps be dated in August 1856, assuming that one of them served for the freshly painted "magnificent angel" of the *Heliodorus*, reported to have been seen then.[44] These beautiful figure drawings are especially remarkable for their anatomical detail, after the many studies of gesture, and correspond to the relative isolation of the figures in the final version.

Not until late in 1859 did Delacroix resume intensive work at the chapel. A sketch in oil, probably one painted for Dutilleux's friend Legentil, which was "almost finished" on April 14, 1860, illustrates the 1860 phase of the *Heliodorus* and closely resembles the mural except in the lower right.[45] Curiously, while this late work has the dramatic forms and flickering light common to the earlier oil sketches, many of the details point to the less vehement final version; most obviously, the rider now has a baton instead of a spear, and his menacing gesture begins to be transformed into one of serene command. Other details of placement and space are different from the mural.[46]

Probably at this time Delacroix made the two sketches of Heliodorus on the sheet owned by the Bremen Museum and formerly in the Riesener Collection (Fig. 63). Here his body is at last rotated almost frontally, as in the final version. The Greco-Roman floral ornaments on his armor are midway between those on the *Trajan* of 1840 and those in the mural.

The Robaut Catalogue, No. 1786, assigns the Fribourg sketch to 1857, without giving a reason.

44. See Adolphe Moreau, *Eugène Delacroix et son oeuvre*, Paris, 1873, xiv. For further discussion of Moreau, see the following section of this chapter. Jacqueline Bouchot-Saupique has published the drawings of the cavalier and of the plunging angel in "Some Drawings by Delacroix in the Musée de Besançon," *Master Drawings*, Autumn 1963, 40-43, pls. 30 and 31. One is struck by the similarity in pose and treatment between the "Study of a Blacksmith" (her pl. 28) for a figure in the frieze *War* at the Salon du Roi, Palais Bourbon (completed in 1835), and the drawing of the cavalier; here, as elsewhere, the artist has transformed motifs borrowed from himself. A fourth study of a nude, for the figure of Heliodorus, belongs both in quality and degree of finish with the three sketches at Besançon. I have seen only a reproduction of this sketch, in the *Catalogue de la vente de Mme. L. Bénédite...*, Hôtel Drouot, 31 May 1928, No. 89.

45. This sketch is illustrated in Escholier, *Delacroix*, III, 96, and by Moreau-Nélaton, *Delacroix raconté*, II, facing p. 196. Moreau-Nélaton says on p. 195 of vol. II that before leaving Paris for the country, in 1860, Delacroix "...made a sketch of his *Heliodorus* (Fig. 414), a canvas worthy of passing into the hands of an artist like Dutilleux, for whom it was intended...." For details about Delacroix's work on the project at this time, see below, next section.

46. The dais is still too short on the right side, and the foreground soldier, who is unlike his counterpart in the mural both in posture and in appearance, crowds the foreground and covers the dais to the right of Heliodorus. Even the Fogg and Chantilly drawings had already placed the foreground soldier closer to the frame and further from the right-hand whipping angel; indeed, the Fogg sketch even hinted at Delacroix's solution to the empty space thus created, by adding a soldier between Heliodorus and the foreground soldier. The levels of the landing and of the balcony in this sketch differ appreciably from the finished version, where the artist left greater space between the figures below and the balcony above.

60 Delacroix, Sketch for the *Heliodorus*. Besançon, Musée des Beaux-Arts et d'Archéologie, No. D2397
(photo: Service de documentation photographique, de la réunion des musées nationaux)

61 Delacroix, Sketch for the *Heliodorus*. Besançon, Musée des Beaux-Arts et d'Archéologie, No. 2426 (photo: Service de documentation photographique, de la réunion des musées nationaux)

62 Delacroix, Sketch for the *Heliodorus*. Besançon, Musée des Beaux-Arts et d'Archéologie, No. D2398 (photo: Service de documentation photographique, de la réunion des musées nationaux)

63 Delacroix, Sketch for the *Heliodorus*. Bremen, Kunsthalle

A sketch from the Louvre (Fig. 64) and its verso (Fig. 65) contain designs for the frame which do not appear before the Dutilleux sketch, and which were probably sketched early in April 1860 as guides for Delacroix's helper Boulangé.[47] There is also a drawing illustrating two-point perspective and ornamental details grouped in bands, probably intended for the frames. The verso has two drawings for ornaments of the frame, as well as a design for the vase in the left corner which appeared in the Dutilleux sketch and not earlier, and which has the following inscription beside it: "dans les coins."[48]

In the last year of work, 1861, Delacroix made a striking change in the lower right corner by moving the foreground soldier closer to the frame, in a different posture. This left a space in the region of the dais, which he filled by placing another soldier in the space vacated by the foreground soldier and by setting a censer on the dais. One of his sketches (Fig. 66) permits us to follow the evolution of the foreground soldier through two positions to that of the mural.[49]

The last sketch (Fig. 67), a drawing of a censer, bears the inscription, "16 mars 61." This object serves to fill some of the enlarged space to the right of Heliodorus and to link the plane of the dais and the first tread down from it. The introduction of this new form is connected with the transformation of the foreground soldier, the addition of a soldier between Heliodorus and the foreground soldier, and the placement of a platter along the lowest step of the dais just below Heliodorus' right leg. All of these very late changes helped to unify the composition by tightening the spaces and interlocking the forms.

B. THE DAY-TO-DAY DEVELOPMENT OF THE MURALS[50]

The long and checkered history of Delacroix's projects to decorate Saint-Sulpice began on January 23, 1847, when the name of the church came up for the first time in the *Journal*,[51] together with various subjects for the transepts.[52] Delacroix entered nothing more in his 1847 *Journal*, probably because negotiations slackened during this prerevolutionary period and did not pass the tentative stage until late in 1848. The next information the *Journal* gives us is that

47. See the *Journal*, April 6, 1860: "I gave him [Boulangé] the idea for the frames."
48. This inscription may refer equally well to the two vases and to the serpent or to the interlaced frame motif behind the serpent. Perhaps at this point Delacroix considered placing a serpent in each corner of the frame, an idea eliminated in the final solution, where the frame decoration resembles the interlace pattern of this sketch.
49. In the drawing at the left the soldier is in profile, as in the earlier sketches, and raises his right arm. The drawing at the right is closer to the finished version and shows the twist of the body, the foreshortened left arm, the right arm raised

overhead and the right knee pointing up. Both sketches differ from the mural in the upturned angle of the soldier's head, which faces down in the finished version.
50. The important illustrated volume of Sérullaz, *Les peintures murales de Delacroix*, includes many of the pertinent writings of the artist together with hitherto unpublished documents from the Archives Nationales, arranged carefully in chronological sequence.
51. All references are to the *Journal*, ed. Joubin.
52. On the day before, January 22, 1847, Delacroix noted in his *Journal* that he had been to see M. Cavé, then Chief of the Division of Fine Arts

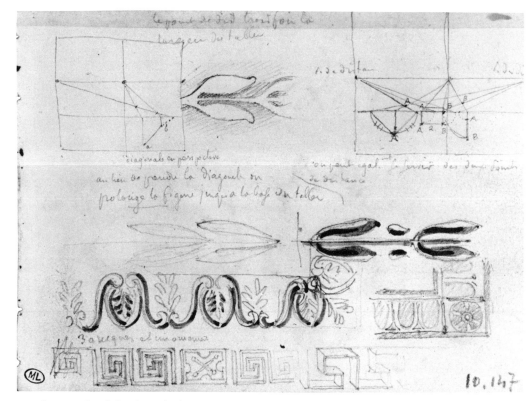

64 Delacroix, Sketch for the *Heliodorus*. Paris, Louvre, RF 10,147r

65 Delacroix, Sketch for the *Heliodorus*. Paris, Louvre, RF 10,147v

66 Delacroix, Sketch for the *Heliodorus*. Paris, Louvre, RF 24,213

67 Delacroix, Sketch for the *Heliodorus*, Paris, Louvre, RF 9523

on January 31 and on February 1, 1849, Mercey, Chief of the Section of Fine Arts, spoke with Delacroix on the matter of Saint-Sulpice.[53] Evidently the preparation of the chapel was seriously under way now, for on March 2, 1849 Delacroix noted: "Went down to Saint-Sulpice and visited the chapel. The ornamentation will be difficult without gilding."

A glimpse into the negotiations—which then concerned the Chapelle des Fonts Baptismaux and no longer the transepts[54]—is provided by a document addressed by the Minister of the Interior to the Prefect of the Seine:[55] "Under the last administration there was question of entrusting to Eugène Delacroix, who had just finished his remarkable paintings of the Library of the Chambre des Députés, the decoration of the Chapelle des Fonts Baptismaux." But, the letter continues, the cost of the chapel (20,000 francs) was too high for the Ministry alone to pay, and negotiations were under way "with your predecessors to find out in what proportion they would help with this expenditure. With the arrival of the Revolution of February, the painting of this project was adjourned." The talents of Delacroix make resumption of the project desirable, and so the letter concludes with a proposal that each pay half, or 10,000 francs, a sum "placed by me on the account of the 1849 and 1850 budgets."

On February 28, 1849 a similar letter was sent by the Minister of the Interior to the Prefect of the Seine. Before replying, the Prefect had V. Baltard[56] prepare, on March 19,1849, a statement listing costs for various materials and work in the Chapelle des Fonts Baptismaux. The walls were to be primed "with boiling oil and basic carbonate of lead *(blanc de céruse)*." Baltard's sum, 6,826 fr. 27 c, added to the 20,000 francs for Delacroix, then made a total of 26,826 fr. 27 c.[57] In his reply of March 22, 1849 to the Minister, the Prefect Berger accepted Delacroix, "there being no objection that can be raised against the choice of this artist," but he pointed out that he had meanwhile consulted the architect's statement of costs for accessory

---

under the Minister of the Interior, probably with his commission in mind. The subjects listed in the *Journal* for January 23, 1847 for the transepts are: Assumption, Ascension, Moses Receiving the Tables of the Law, Moses on the Mountain, Deluge, Tower of Babel, Apocalypse, Crucifixion, The Angel Destroying the Assyrian Army, The Carrying of the Cross, The Entombment.

53. See the *Journal* for these dates. Mercey served under Charles Blanc, new Chief of the Division of Fine Arts, replacing Cavé. The year 1848 is missing. See *Journal*, I, xi.

54. The Chapelle des Fonts Baptismaux was located next to the north tower and became later the Chapelle de Saint François Xavier, decorated in 1853-59 by E. Lafon. The transepts were not to

be decorated until 1876 by Signol with the themes of Judas' Betrayal, Jesus' Death, Resurrection, and Ascension. On these points see Gaston Lemesle, *L'Eglise Saint-Sulpice*, Paris, 1931, **94** and 155f.

55. *Archives nationales*, Paris, 5th ser., F²¹ 24, dated "Paris, le...184...." This document is undated, but probably was written between December 1848 and February 1849 since there is a reference to the "last administration."

56. Victor Baltard (1805-74), the Director of Works for Paris and the Department of the Seine, built Les Halles and Saint-Augustin, and was very active in supervising church decoration. Delacroix held no high opinion of his ability. See the *Journal*, September 28, 1853.

works and found that the total to be paid was now 26,826 fr. 27 c, not 20,000 francs.[58]

On April 10, 1849 the *Journal* lists subjects for Delacroix's project in "the chapel of Saint-Sulpice": "The Archangel St. Michael Throwing Down the Devil;[59] for the ceiling or pendentives: Jesus Drawing Souls from Purgatory; again for the pendentives: The Original Sin or Adam and Eve after the Fall;[60] for the ceiling: Christ's Descent to Limbo." The same day Delacroix visited the Chapelle des Fonts Baptismaux at Notre Dame de Lorette to view its subjects, and of what he saw there he listed: "Christ Rising from the Tomb, Christ Conqueror of Death and Sin, Preaching of St. John, Christianity Preached to the Indians, and Christ Preaching in the Barque."

On April 28, 1849 a document from the Director of Fine Arts at the Ministry of the Interior, 5th Division, Charles Blanc[61] (who did not sign his name), to the Prefect of the Seine, referred to the new figure, 26,826 fr. 27 c, a sum which "is not at all excessive" in view of the chapel's importance. He added that "the rare merit with which M. E. Delacroix has executed the murals decorating the former Throne Room" (which had been renamed Salon du Roi and which is now called Salon Delacroix) "and the Library of the Chamber of Deputies offers the Administration sufficient guarantee of the care which he will take in executing this work, and would warrant you to entrust it to him."[62]

On May 20, 1849 Delacroix recorded in the *Journal*—probably intending to enter it on May 21—receipt of notification from the Ministry of the Interior of the commission for Saint-Sulpice, still referring to the Chapelle des Fonts Baptismaux. The letter addressed to him by the Ministry of the Interior to inform him of the commission actually bears the date May 21, 1849.[63] Delacroix was probably informed unofficially before this date by the City of Paris, through Varcollier, head of the Division of Fine Arts in the Prefecture of the Seine; for the

57. This important unpublished document, *Archives nationales*, Paris, 5th ser., F²¹ 24, states that "Les travaux consistent dans l'établissement d'un échafaud, le dressement des murs des voûtes et leur préparation pour recevoir les peintures; la peinture de décor...."

58. *Archives nationales*, Paris, 5th ser., F²¹ 24.

59. The only theme in the group actually executed.

60. Both were treated by Adolphe Roger in the Chapelle du Baptême in Notre Dame de Lorette in 1840.

61. Charles Blanc (1813-82), the influential art critic, writer and engraver, was Director of Fine Arts from 1848 to 1852, and from 1870 to 1873. He helped keep Delacroix's commission for Saint-Sulpice alive during the Second Republic.

62. *Archives nationales*, Paris, 5th ser., F²¹ 24. Sérullaz, *Les peintures*, 150, gives the text of the last sentence (in part) as "...du soin qu'il mettra à exécuter ce travail et vous (un mot illisible) à le lui confier." In my reading of this text, the "mot illisible" is given as "autoriserait," which seems to fit. In its letter dated the same day as Blanc's, April 28, 1849, the Ministry of the Interior announced that "M. Eugène Delacroix is charged to execute...for 13,413 francs...the mural paintings which are to decorate the Chapelle des Fonts Baptismaux in the church of St. Sulpice, Paris," *Archives nationales*, same series.

63. *Archives nationales*, same series. Sérullaz, *Les peintures*, 151, first observed the misdating by Delacroix.

same entry mentions that several days before he had been to Varcollier "to thank him." On May 23, 1849 Delacroix sent a letter to Charles Blanc to thank him for his help in securing the Saint-Sulpice commission.[64]

In his entries of May 31 and June 2, 1849 Delacroix listed subjects, many of them religious, and while he used none of them for Saint-Sulpice, his interest in the mural project probably led him to proliferate religious subjects.[65]

The Chapelle des Saints-Anges at last entered the records on August 10, 1849, for on that day the City of Paris issued an order charging Delacroix to decorate the chapel.[66] There was much confusion as to which chapel the artist was to decorate, and sixteen days later a newspaper article reported that Delacroix was "charged to execute the great fresco at Saint-Sulpice, in the Chapelle des Fonts Baptismaux."[67] The question has also been raised recently as to whether the two chapels were really only one chapel with its name changed. My view is that two distinct chapels were involved, the rejected one beside the north tower and the decorated one beside the south tower.[68] I believe, therefore, that the uncertainties he described in a letter on August 31, 1849 to Lassalle-Bordes,[69] his assistant, and the difficulties and changes occur-

64. All references to Delacroix's correspondence are to the *Correspondance générale*, ed. Joubin. The letter to Blanc is in vol. II, p. 391. Sérullaz, *Les peintures*, 153, has sensibly corrected the date given by Joubin—August 23, 1849—to May 23, 1849, and I have followed him in this. The letter is inscribed "ce 23," with no month, but should be placed just after Delacroix's receipt of notification of the commission on May 21.

65. Cf. the entries in the *Journal* on April 10, October 6 and October 16, 1849.

66. *Archives nationales*, Paris, 5th ser., F²¹ 24. This is known from a note dated June 27, 1859, of Baltard, which reads: "...E. Delacroix, chargé par arrêté en date du 10 Août 1849 de l'exécution des peintures murales pour la décoration de la Chapelle des Saints-Anges...."

67. *Le pays, journal des volontés de la France*, August 26, 1849, No. 235, p. 2, col. 2.

68. Sérullaz, *Les peintures*, 149, 152, returning to a view earlier offered by Maurice Tourneux, *Delacroix*, Paris, n.d., 75, corrects Joubin's opinion that there were two different chapels involved in the negotiations, the Chapelle des Fonts Baptismaux and the Chapelle des Saints-Anges. Sérullaz tries to demonstrate that there was a Chapelle des Fonts Baptismaux whose name was changed to Chapelle des Saints-Anges and that they are one and the same. I do not agree with his demon-

stration. Gaston Lemesle, *L'Eglise Saint-Sulpice*, Paris, 1931 (?), 187, pointed out, referring to the present Chapelle des Saints-Anges: "En 1844, on la mît sous l'invocation des Saints Anges...." This was the same chapel beside the south tower which Delacroix decorated. The chapel on the left beside the north tower directly opposite the present Chapelle des Saints-Anges was originally to have been the Chapelle des Fonts Baptismaux. I believe that the artist's difficulties in August and September 1849 concerned not different chapels but different subjects for the Chapelle des Saints-Anges. For further explanation see Lemesle, *L'Eglise Saint-Sulpice*, 154.

69. Gustave Lassalle-Bordes (1815-?), Delacroix's main collaborator on the decorations of the Chamber of Deputies and the Senate, later fell out with the master and was not hired to help at Saint-Sulpice. Joubin has noted that Delacroix was dissatisfied already with Lassalle-Bordes and began putting him off while he found other helpers, e.g. Andrieu, with whom he had already worked. The manuscripts of Lassalle-Bordes, who worked long and closely with Delacroix, contain, despite their rancor and occasional distortion, valuable notes on Delacroix's ways of working. Baudelaire discussed Lassalle-Bordes's *The Death of Cleopatra* in his *Salon of 1845*.

ring in September 1849 concerned not the question of which chapel but which subjects he would execute.[70] He and the curé (Abbé Collin) could not agree on subjects, which must have been especially irritating then; for, as Delacroix wrote in a letter of September 17, 1849 to his friend Riesener, he had already completed his compositions.[71] After continuing his search for subjects,[72] on October 2, 1849 he and the curé came to an agreement: "Today I finally came to a decision with the curé and his vicar M. Goujon that I will do the Holy Angels, and I notice that it is the very day of their festival that I have accepted this agreement."[73] By January 22, 1850 Delacroix referred, in a letter to Lassalle-Bordes, to the first of his definitive subjects for the chapel, St. Michael Vanquishing Lucifer. On February 27, 1850, according to the *Journal*, he worked on his sketches to submit to the Prefecture, the key judge in all questions concerning monumental decoration (as pointed out in Chapter I), and by March of the same year he showed his helper the finished sketches for the three paintings.[74]

Delacroix turned to technical and artistic questions soon after October 2, 1849, when the difficulties over the commission were resolved. Already on February 4, 1850 he wrote in his *Journal* that he wanted "frames of white marble around the paintings; next frames of red or

70. A *Journal* entry of September 1, 1849 (Champrosay) reads: "...the letter of the architect Baltard informs me of the necessity to change my subjects for Saint-Sulpice." This difficulty occasioned a complaint to his old friend Mme. de Forget in his letter of September 10, 1849, which tells of his uncertainty with regard to the painting of the chapel. Probably such uncertainties can in part be traced back to the confusions between City and State in the assignment of commissions. Cf. Chapter I, note 18.

71. A letter to Lassalle-Bordes of January 22, 1850 summed up the situation: "Here is what happened. The chapel was that of the baptismal fonts. The subjects came easily: baptism, original sin, expiation, etc. I got the consent of the curé and composed my paintings. At the end of three months I receive a letter in the country which informs me that the Chapelle des Fonts Baptismaux is found under the porch of the church rather than in the place I was supposed to paint; it is this error...which has kept me in suspense since September....At last, I believe we'll definitely consecrate the Chapelle des Saints-Anges. There are suitable subjects. The ceiling will be *St. Michael Vanquishing Lucifer.*" According to an earlier letter to Lassalle-Bordes, of November 16, 1849, Delacroix was by this time only prevented from completing prepara-

tory work in the chapel because his helper (Lassalle-Bordes) had been bitten by a dog and incapacitated.

72. See the *Journal* for September 28, 1849 (Champrosay): "I looked for the big Bible; spoke a lot about subjects."

73. At the top of the page of the original manuscript of the *Journal* for October 2, 1849 are printed the words: "Ss. Anges Gardiens." Delacroix had intended to confer with the curé on the day before for his subjects but postponed the meeting. See the *Journal*, October 1, 1849.

74. See Lassalle-Bordes's letter to Burty of June 20, 1879, at the Institut d'Art et d'Archéologie, Paris, MS 245, 21. If, as the letter states, Lassalle-Bordes saw the sketches in March, then Delacroix must have decided finally against hiring him shortly afterwards; for a letter of May 7, 1850 from Champrosay to the uncle of Pierre Andrieu—destined to replace Lassalle-Bordes— proposed that the uncle allow his nephew to work with him on Delacroix's new commission. By December 1, 1850 Delacroix was referring ironically to Lassalle-Bordes's sincerity in a letter to his new helper Andrieu. Although Delacroix had "finished" his sketches in March 1850, he continued to work on them, as he mentioned in a letter from Champrosay of May 19, 1850 to Mme. Babut.

green, as in the Chapel of the Virgin,[75] and a setting for the whole in white with ornaments in stone, imitating gold, like the gilded coppers of the same chapel. (If one could make the frames in white stucco.)"[76] He also mentioned how he wanted the walls primed. At a later date when the priming was actually being done, he gave other details, stating that it was to be of lead carbonate (céruse) and boiling oil.[77]

On a trip to Antwerp, Belgium, in August 1850, Delacroix visited the churches, as he often did at this time, and was reminded of his chapel decoration.[78] When he returned to Paris on October 5, 1850, he wrote joyfully to Dutilleux about his own subjects, which would bring him "side by side with some great masters," adding (with a sentiment more romantic than Catholic) that one of the attractive qualities of religious subjects was that of "allowing full play to the imagination, so that each artist is thereby enabled to express what he feels."

Despite his enthusiasm, the artist does not seem to have actually done any work in the chapel before 1852. However, in his *Journal* he set down on January 2, 1851 the dimensions of his ceiling (5 x 3.84 meters),[79] and on August 14, 1851 he listed subjects "for the pendentives: Angels, one playing a trumpet, the other showing the terrible book—Angels presenting the incense or the votive flame—The candelabrum—Psalms—Guardian angel—Angel leading souls in passage from the body—Angel waking the dead."[80]

Delacroix arranged in October 1851 to have his pupil Andrieu, who had successfully worked with him on the decoration of the Apollo ceiling, collaborate at Saint-Sulpice.[81] From this point on there is no mention of Lassalle-Bordes in connection with the chapel.

During 1852 Delacroix could do little more in the chapel than to sketch in the pendentives in April (see Figs. 68 and 69), while Andrieu seems to have worked in the chapel not more than two days at the beginning of March 1852 and probably two days at the beginning of April; for

75. The Chapel of the Virgin in the apse of Saint-Sulpice was decorated by Lemoyne and Van Loo in the 18th century.

76. Joubin remarks concerning the frames: "In reality, the frames are in imitation gold tints, painted on the wall. Delacroix has therefore changed his mind." Delacroix's original manuscript (MS 253, Institut d'Art et d'Archéologie, Paris) contains a sketch by the artist explaining his idea, which is not reproduced in Joubin's edition of the *Journal*. It shows two concentric bands, curved like the tops of the *Heliodorus* and the *Jacob*, the outer of which is labeled "marbre vert ou rouge," the inner "marbre bleu." Delacroix wrote the word "pierre" twice—once above, and once below these bands.

77. See the *Journal*, June 8, 1850 and letter to Baltard of June 25, 1850. In a letter of June 28, 1850 to Lassalle-Bordes, Delacroix spoke of the priming

then going on, after the rescraping and replastering of the walls, adding that he would be ready to work in the chapel "at the end of August or at the beginning of September." It may be noted that boiling oil on plaster was used at least as far back as Vasari. See *Vasari on Technique*, ed. G. Baldwin Brown, New York, 1960, 232.

78. See the *Journal*, July 7, 1850 and August 2, 3, 5, 8, 9, 11, 12, 1850, etc.

79. Baltard gave the dimensions of the ceiling of the Chapelle des Fonts Baptismaux, which is on the north side, including frame, in his statement of March 19, 1849 in *Archives nationales*, Paris, 5th ser., F²¹ 24: 7.00 x 5.53 meters. He gave the dimensions without frame, in *Archives de la Seine* V 71 M³² 1, note of May 29, 1855, as 5.30 x 4.15 meters.

80. Although Delacroix made sketches of all these angel types, only the angels with book, flame,

the master and Andrieu were absorbed by a new project at the Hôtel de Ville from October 1851 to October 1852, with retouching *in situ* that lasted up till the spring of 1854.[82]

That Delacroix may have tried to begin work in 1853 is suggested by an isolated reference in the *Journal* to the "ceiling of Saint-Sulpice" on September 26, 1853 and a document indicating that a scaffold had been set up in the chapel sometime between December 18, 1852 and December 18, 1853.[83]

Early in 1854 all the surfaces to be painted were completely reprimed.[84] Delacroix wrote to Andrieu on April 24 that "...it would be unwise to work on a wall that is newly primed. The job they've done is excellent because the old priming was so thick that it had no adherence to the wall; they've scratched out everything and put a very light one, after having applied boiling oil anew! I do not believe it is possible to begin again before six weeks at least." On June 15 he noted in the *Journal* that "Andrieu begins at Saint-Sulpice," and on June 25 that what his helper had traced there was "excellent."[85] Enthusiastic, he wrote on June 30 in his *Journal*: "All goes well. My heart beats faster in the presence of great walls to paint." He would have wanted to work Sundays, as he had already done at Saint-Denis-du-Saint-Sacrement, since the music of the services "exalts" and inspires him, and being refused, he exclaimed, perhaps with a touch of irony: "The Emperor, the Empress, His Grace, conspire so that a poor painter like me may not commit the sacrilege of giving free rein, on Sundays as on other days, to the ideas he draws from his hand to glorify The Lord."[86]

During the rest of 1854 Delacroix was absorbed in preparing for the great Universal Exhibition to be held in Paris during 1855, and in which he was to enter 35 paintings. The *Journal* contains only one more entry for 1854, that of October 2, recording that the artist "worked at Saint-Sulpice to draw *Heliodorus* again." Not before May 15, 1855, the day the exhibition

and palms and the one with incense appear in the finished pendentives.

81. On Andrieu see the introduction to this chapter. A letter by Delacroix to Andrieu's uncle, dated October 17, 1851, mentions the new collaboration.

82. See the *Journal*, April 5 and 6, 1852. That Andrieu was probably involved in the work at the chapel at this time is shown by his entries into the *Agenda* of 1852 for April 1. On Andrieu's *Agenda*, see the introduction to this chapter.

83. See the list of costs signed "V. Baltard," *Archives de la Seine*, Paris, V 71 M³² 1, Préfecture du Département de la Seine, Exercice de l'An 1853, ch. 18, art. 3.

84. A memo of works by the Prefecture of the Seine for 1854, signed by Baltard, reads: "First chapel to the right, the circular medallion of the ceiling and the two lateral walls, steeped with siccative oil with aid of fire, sealed with a cement of pure white lead (*céruse*), and painted with white oil as a seal (*tampon*) of the bed of the decoration. ..." A second memo, labeled in the same way, and also signed by Baltard, reads: "Hatchings executed on the walls of the chapel in order to imitate the grain of the canvas (*la toile*) and to receive the paintings of M. Delacroix, from March 19 to March 29, 1854." See Préfecture du Département de la Seine, *Archives de la Seine*, Paris, V 71 M³² 1 ("Mémoire des travaux de peinture exercés à l'Eglise St. Sulpice").

85. Probably the sketch which Delacroix showed to Mercey, the director of the Beaux-Arts, on June 24, 1854, as mentioned in the *Journal*, was for Saint-Sulpice.

86. See the *Journal*, August 3, 1854. He had asked—on June 2, 1854—M. Coquant, Abbé of Saint-Sulpice for permission to work on Sundays.

68 Delacroix, Sketch for the pendentives. Paris, Louvre, RF 9516

69 Robaut's copy of one of Delacroix's drawings for the pendentives. Robaut, *L'Oeuvre complet*, No. 1338

opened, did he refer to the chapel again. In a letter of May 16 he informed Andrieu that they would probably not be able to resume work on the murals before the 15th or 16th of June.

On July 19, 1855, Delacroix met with the architects and painters, with whose priming of the walls he was evidently dissatisfied; for by August 9 he had been hard at work in the chapel for fifteen days,[87] mainly repriming the walls by himself, a task which almost gave him lead poisoning.[88] It is not clear from the available evidence why he was dissatisfied with the priming already on the walls since, as we have just seen, he had found it excellent on April 24, 1854. The *Journal* for August 27 notes that there had been an interruption of the project for the preceding eight days because of his illness and the "frightfully persistent heat," which made the work too painful for him. When he returned to work, he preferred the cooler mornings, and once was inspired by the music of an unusual service given at 8:00 A.M. on August 30, according to his *Journal* for that date.

Delacroix did little more in the chapel until February 23, 1856, when a letter to Andrieu tells us: "We will begin by sketching the ceiling painting over the cartoon which is fastened above, in order to judge the proportions."[89] Soon afterward, a second helper joined the project, Boulangé, to whom Delacroix addressed a letter on March 13, requesting help with the backgrounds of the two lower paintings, an important job "because I cannot continue my figures unless these parts are very advanced."[90] Both helpers worked on the chapel during March,[91] but not on the same days, according to a letter to Boulangé dated March 15, 1856: "I should indeed have asked you to come Monday, if it were possible, and prepare what's necessary, but the person who works with me [Andrieu] will be set up on that day. Once started on Saint-Sulpice we'll take one day to make the canvases on a Sunday, e.g., when they don't permit me to work at the church." These canvases were probably the sections which were to be attached to the ceiling by *marouflage*, the gluing of a canvas to its support, which was the commonest alternative to fresco.

87. See the letter to George Sand of July 19 and one to Louis Guillemardet of August 9.

88. See his letter to Dutilleux, September 8, 1855.

89. This letter also refers to "M. Haro's" having been in the chapel. It is probable that the technical expert Haro had given advice concerning the *marouflage*, or gluing of the canvas to the ceiling.

90. Louis Boulangé (1812-78), a former pupil of Delacroix, as well as of the famous stage designer Cicéri (not to be confused with Louis Boulanger [1806-67]), had collaborated on the backgrounds of the *Trajan* and of the *Entry of the Crusaders into Constantinople*. See Joubin's note in the *Journal*, III, 533, Supplement.

91. See the *Journal* for March 17, 20, 21, and 22.

92. On the scaffolding, see *Archives de la Seine*, Paris, V 71 M³² 1, Exercice 1856.

93. See the *Journal* for May 18 and 19.

94. See the letters to Haro, June 15, 1856, and to his cousin Auguste Lamey on June 22, 1856; and the *Journal* for July 28, 1856.

95. See the undated letter (which Joubin puts in August) to his old friend Baron Louis de Schwiter, an amateur painter (1809-65); and a memo of August 20, 1856 with Baltard's name on it, *Archives de la Seine*, Paris, V 71 M³² 1, Exercice 1856.

96. Moreau, *Eugène Delacroix et son oeuvre*, xiv. Adolphe Moreau was a wealthy stockbroker whose great collection of Delacroix paintings was given to the Louvre by his son, Etienne

On April 20 a movable scaffolding was placed in the chapel, and by May 6 Delacroix recorded in his *Journal* that "We are drawing the cartoon of the ceiling."[92] On May 19 the paper pasteboards *(cartons)* which Haro provided were put behind the painting.[93] After this intense activity, there was a lapse of several weeks of idleness, and while Delacroix complained about "falling behind" in his work, Andrieu continued alone in the chapel from June 17 to July 17, to be rejoined by the master on July 28.[94] August, with its "beautiful days for work" was very productive, and changes in the scaffolding were made to facilitate it.[95]

Probably at about this time Moreau made his revealing visit to the chapel.[96] "I remember ...," wrote Moreau, "... that one day in the month of August 1856, visiting with Delacroix his frescos of Saint-Sulpice, still enveloped by their covering of boards, he obligingly showed us this magnificent angel which, in the painting of *Heliodorus*, strikes the profaner with vengeful scourge. The fragment had hardly been finished, and the master attributed its exceptional success to the indefinable state of mind into which the sounds of the organ playing *Dies Irae* had plunged him."

Perhaps rushing before "the uncertain light of the end of autumn" would force him to quit the chapel,[97] Delacroix, "leading the life of a cenobite," worked intensively on the *Jacob* and "raised the tone of the whole group *(remonté)*," etc.[98] On the last day of the campaign, September 25, 1856, the artist worked on the angels for the pendentives which had been primed during the year.[99] While winter compelled him to lay aside his own work, he tried to arrange with Boulangé to resume work on the chapel ornaments.[100] Then Delacroix became ill, and from December 1856 to March 1857, he was unable to work even in his studio.[101]

For a whole year his sickness kept him from Saint-Sulpice, although he does seem to have worked in his studio, perhaps on the sketches for the *Jacob*, and on a copy of the *St. Michael*.[102] During the summer he began moving to a new studio at 6, Rue Furstenberg, his last one, which he entered on December 28, 1857. On July 3, 1858 he finally began working at the church with Andrieu, but by August 11, 1858 his health again forced him to stop, and he left Paris for

Moreau-Nélaton. Moreau's visit was perhaps not exceptional, for the public knew of Delacroix's labors in his chapel. This fact was mentioned, e.g. in Gustave Planche's article "La peinture murale," *Revue des deux mondes*, 6, 1856, 44-75.

97. See the letter of August 24, 1856 to Dutilleux.

98. See the *Journal*, August 26, 1856, in the Pach translation, and August 27, 1856.

99. See the *Journal*, September 25, 1856. For the priming of the pendentives, see Baltard's memo in *Archives de la Seine*, Paris, V 71 M^{32} 1, Préfecture de la Seine, Exercice 1856.

100. See the letters to Lamey of November 8, 1856, to Boulangé of November 30, and to an anonymous addressee on "Friday 19" (dated in December 1856 by Joubin, *Correspondance générale*, III, 349).

101. See the letter to Dutilleux, March 5, 1857.

102. See the *Journal*, April 25, 1857, which gives the biblical text preceding the main episode: "Jacob divided in two flocks his servants, his sheep, his cows, and his camels. Thirty camels with their sucklings made part of the presents directed to his brother in the hope to appease him." Probably Delacroix was then focusing on the forms in the caravan on the right side of his painting, and may have sketched details of it. On the copy of the *St. Michael* requested by Dutilleux for his friend Legentil of Arras, see the *Journal*, March 27, 1856 and letter to Dutilleux, January 30, 1858.

Champrosay.[103] On September 5, shortly before his return to Paris, Delacroix made an important note in his *Journal* on the technique of gluing paper, which indicates that the canvas for the *St. Michael* had evidently not yet been attached to the ceiling.[104]

On September 11, 1858 some work on the *Heliodorus* inaugurated a new campaign, which, despite momentary relapses, proceeded with energy and ended only on the approach of cold, when darkness chased him from the chapel, but not without "the hope of finishing this year."[105] Actually, Delacroix had come quite close to completing his work, having "terminated the first draft," as Baltard acknowledged, and he began pressing both the City and the State for payment.[106] This pressure was in part successful, for the State paid 5,000 francs in 1859.[107] By January 2, 1860 he received the balance of the 10,000 francs owed by the State, and Baltard had already notified the Ministry, in a letter of December 27, 1859, that the City had still paid only 5,000 francs.[108]

After returning from a trip to Strasbourg in September, Delacroix threw himself "body and soul" into his decorations; and, discontented with his progress, he arranged to work in the chapel during the winter.[109] In March 1860 he engaged Boulangé to work on the ornaments, with the agreement of M. Denuelle, Superintendent of Works.[110] Boulangé's work did not satisfy the artist, who noted in his *Journal* on April 6: "I was at Saint-Sulpice today. Boulangé has done nothing and has not understood a word of what I said. I gave him the idea of the frames in grisaille[111] and of the garland, brush in hand, and with fury. Astonishing thing! I came back tired and not enervated. It seems to me that I have recovered my health, after so many relapses." This demonstration only seems to have irritated the helper, who broke an appointment to come to the chapel on the next day, but did return by April 9.[112] Delacroix's impatience with the decorators[113] who in his absence "would do a thousand silly things," occasioned a caustic letter to Boulangé on April 28. But some of the errors were due to his own mis-

103. Cf. a letter to his cousin Mme. de Forget, dated August 31, from Champrosay.
104. "Villot tells me to glue paper on the vault of my chapel before gluing the painting. That is practiced by the decorators and strongly recommended." Cf. also *Journal*, May 18, 1856.
105. See the *Journal*, September 11, 1858, letters to Berryer, October 4, to Lamey, October 6, to his friend Paul Huet (1803-67, the landscape painter), October 13, 1858, and to Dutilleux, January 3, 1859. Later, in two letters to Lamey of May 26 and June 24, 1859, he repeated his hopes of finishing.
106. Baltard's note of June 27, 1859 requested the City to pay the artist 5,000 fr. on account. See *Archives nationales*, Paris, 5th ser., F²¹ 24.
107. Delacroix's letter of July 12, 1859 to Alfred Arago, inspector of Fine Arts for the Ministry of State indicates that he had only received 5,000 fr. from the State.
108. The memo of January 2, 1860 by the Director of Fine Arts for the Ministry of State, is in the *Archives nationales*, Paris, 5th ser., F²¹ 24. Baltard's note is in the same archive, as is one of December 26, 1859 to the same effect, but with fewer details.
109. See letters to Lamey, September 15 and October 17, 1859, and to Baudelaire, December 13, 1859.
110. Delacroix first wrote to Boulangé about the decorations on February 15, 1860 and later on March 13, 1860, after consulting with M. Denuelle. Alexandre Denuelle (1818-79), himself a painter, worked with the Commission on Historical Monuments.

judgments, one of which he admitted in a letter to Boulangé on May 14, 1860. The correction of such errors particularly annoyed Delacroix since he feared that he might have to pay for the ornaments himself, the credit allocated to him for the decoration being almost exhausted; furthermore, an extra cost had resulted from damages to the garlands by humidity.[114]

Although by April 1860 his work had entered "its most interesting phase" (the final one, of retouching), from June to October Delacroix, hindered by ill health and fatigue, could do little beyond directing Andrieu's work.[115] He would undertake something in the chapel, and then go off to Champrosay to recuperate.[116] In order to restore his health and to facilitate his work, he lived soberly and worked on a schedule, a style of life which he called "a bit odd, considering my usual indolence."[117] On November 13 he wrote to Andrieu from Champrosay directing him to continue with the ceiling, where there was still much to do. He himself stayed on the project to the end of December, despite a bad cold and "the dimness of the light."[118]

In high spirits Delacroix launched his last year in the chapel on January 1, 1861 with the famous passage from his *Journal:* "I've begun this year pursuing my work at the church as usual; I've made no visits except by cards, which don't distract me at all, and I've been working the whole day; happy life! Heavenly compensation for my pretended isolation!...for four months I flee during the dawn and run to this enchanting work as to the feet of the dearest mistress; what seemed easy to surmount from afar presents me with horrible and incessant difficulties. But how is it that this eternal combat, instead of beating me down, elevates me, instead of discouraging me, consoles me and fills my moments, when I've left it?..."[119]

By early May the end was in sight, and Delacroix, hastening to open the chapel before the end of the Salon, pressed Boulangé to finish quickly his gold garland, the uprights, and the grisailles against the window "with simple glazes."[120] But his "drudgery" dragged through July, when at long last, after ten months of uninterrupted work, he began to apply the finishing

111. The frames in grisaille were to serve as links between the *St. Michael* and the pendentives.

112. See the *Journal* for April 7 and April 9, 1860.

113. There were several decorators either assigned by the City or commissioned by Delacroix to help Boulangé with the minor but laborious work on the ornaments.

114. See *Journal,* April 10, 1860.

115. See the letter to Baron de Schwiter, April 30, 1860, and the letters to Lamey, June 25 and August 13.

116. See the letter to Haro, September 10, 1860, and to Léon Riesener (1808-78, painter and cousin of Delacroix), October 7, 1860.

117. See letters to Berryer, October 14, 1860, to P. Huet, October 30, 1860, and to Soulier, November 10, 1860.

118. See the *Journal,* November 25, 1860, and a letter to Berryer, December 4, 1860.

119. The next paragraph speaks of "yellow highlights in the flesh," and is probably associated with his current work of putting finishing touches to the murals. This is particularly interesting because Delacroix so rarely discussed his decoration of the chapel in technical terms. He referred also in this entry to Rubens' *Kermesse,* perhaps because he was at the time working on the *Jacob,* which also has figures in a landscape setting. On his high spirits, cf. his letter to George Sand, January 12, 1861.

120. See the letter to Boulangé of May 7, 1861.

touches.[121] On July 23, 1861, before he actually finished, he sent a note to Charles Blanc, inviting him to visit the chapel and thanking him for his help in getting the commission.

The official invitation, dated July 29,[122] reads: "M. Delacroix begs you to be good enough to do him the honor of visiting the works he has just finished in the Chapelle des Saints-Anges at Saint-Sulpice. These works may be seen by means of this letter, from Wednesday, July 31, to Saturday, August 3, inclusive, from 1:00 to 5:00 in the afternoon. First chapel to the right on entering through the main portal." Selected persons received a copy, which would admit them before the chapel was open to the public, among them: Théophile Gautier (July 1861); Paul de Saint-Victor (July 22, 1861); Charles Blanc (July 23, 1861); Achille Fould, Minister of State; Baron Haussmann, Préfet; Mme. de Forget, and Thiers (all on July 29, 1861); Thoré (July 30, 1861).

Even after sending out this invitation, Delacroix was not yet through; for the next day he had to retouch some slight damages to the paintings "from the brusk removal of the scaffolding."[123] But then his long campaign to finish the chapel, which had kept him out of his studio for the ten months from October 1860 to July 1861, was over, and on August 5 he could write to Alfred Arago, requesting the balance of payment due him. This was ordered to be paid on August 9, 1861 by the Chief of the Division of Fine Arts at the Ministry of State, and amounted to 3,413 francs for the incidental costs which the artist had himself laid out (e.g. to workmen, etc., exclusive of the two helpers).[124] The enclosure was taken down, and the public admitted on August 21, 1861.[125]

The chapel was visited chiefly by appreciative artists, which apparently more than made up for the disappointing absence of "big-wigs": "I have had a visit neither from the Minister, nor the Prefect, nor Nieuwerkerke, nor anyone from the Court, nor persons of rank, despite my invitations. As for the 'gentlemen of the Institute,' they have come in very small numbers; but, on the other hand, many artists have come. Moreover, there were few people in Paris. In sum, I am happy; on all sides they assure me that I am not yet dead."[126]

On September 27, 1861, the Fine Arts Commission of the City of Paris reported on having had Delacroix's paintings examined by a subcommission, and noted: "This work has seemed to the subcommission worthy of the former works of this artist. It has been treated with con-

121. See the letters to his friend Louis Guillemardet of May 22, 1861, to Burty of July 19, and to Paul de Saint-Victor of July 22, 1861.

122. Given correctly by Sérullaz, *Les peintures*, 164, for the first time.

123. See the invitations to Haussmann, July 29, 1861, and to Thoré, July 30, 1861.

124. *Archives nationales*, Paris, 5th ser., F²¹ 24. The Ministry of State referred here to the Chapelle des Fonts Baptismaux. This confusion of the two chapels, after the change was concluded, occurred more than once in the State's memoranda, but was never made by the City, whose architect Baltard worked in the chapel from the beginning.

scientiousness and talent."[127] Interesting in the light of the controversial character of Delacroix's art is the fact that the words which immediately follow—in the same ink as the rest of the manuscript—are crossed out in the draft of the manuscript in the archives: "...and can be considered as a complete specimen of the brilliant qualities of the illustrious colorist."

Now that it was all over, Delacroix, in a nostalgic mood, wrote to Andrieu on October 17, 1861, indicating his readiness to begin another mural: "It seems to me that we finished our work a long time ago. I've forgotten the enormous pains it has given to me." With the prospect of future commissions in mind, he advised his helper: "Work, profit from every moment: and if the administration favors me, perhaps we'll experience once more some of the disappointments and hopes of our former sessions."

On the payment of Boulangé through Baltard see Delacroix's letter to Boulangé on September 1, 1861.

125. See the letter to Thoré, and the one to Blanc, whom the artist regretted not seeing when he visited the chapel, both letters dated August 23, 1861.

126. See the letters to Boulangé and to Riesener, both of September 1, 1861.

127. *Archives de la Seine*, Paris, VR (Beaux-Arts de la Ville), No. 160 (versement 7138), Commission des Beaux-Arts 1859-70.

III. THE MURALS

A. THE SUBJECTS

On October 2, 1849, when Delacroix and the curé held their interview at Saint-Sulpice, they agreed conclusively on the three subjects for the chapel decoration, as we have seen. One of them, St. Michael, seems to have attracted the artist for its engagement of a winged angel and an adversary; indeed, he presented variants of the same idea in his other two paintings. Delacroix's version—as his contemporaries often remarked—clearly resembles the large Renaissance painting of the same theme in the Louvre, then as now attributed by the museum to Raphael, assisted by Giuliano Romano.[1] It was noted in Chapter II that Delacroix had already included St. Michael in a group of subjects for the Chapelle des Fonts Baptismaux. Apparently without having in mind a definite program for the chapel, he listed it among various subjects "for the ceiling or in the chapel or for one of the pendentives"; however, when the chapel was definitively changed to that of the Saints-Anges, only the subject of St. Michael survived. The curé who had refused Delacroix's other proposals probably did not object to this one; indeed, a painting of the same theme by Rémond (1827) had already hung in the old Chapelle des Fonts Baptismaux.[2] In his letter to Lassalle-Bordes of January 22, 1850, Delacroix referred to St. Michael as the subject intended for his ceiling, with no mention yet of Jacob or Heliodorus.

The choice of Jacob by the artist depended in part on an interest antedating his actual commission. He had already considered it in relation to a mural enterprise,[3] so that it probably occurred quite naturally to him in connection with a chapel dedicated to the guardian angels.[4] Characteristically, the artist interpreted the biblical episode not as a moment of triumph and blessing, but as one of painful struggle; indeed, his published description of the scene concludes

1. The small *St. Michael* by Raphael in the Louvre is not in question, for Delacroix's version does not resemble it.
2. Rémond's painting, titled *Saint-Michel terrassant le Démon*, is now in the Sacristy of Marriages. See Lemesle, *L'Eglise Saint-Sulpice*, 165.
3. A list of unexecuted mural subjects for the Palais Bourbon, painted in 1838-47, contains "La Lutte de Jacob et de l'Ange." See *Journal*, III, 380, n.d.
4. Tobias and the Angel, a subject resembling the theme of the guardian angel, might also have occurred to Delacroix, especially since he had recently copied Titian's version of it. See *Journal*, December 15, 1847. In the 18th century Giannantonio or Francesco Guardi executed a celebrated series of paintings based on the theme of Tobias. Possibly Delacroix rejected it as lacking the potential for monumentality or dramatic force to which he aspired.
5. Delacroix's note announcing the opening of his chapel on July 29, 1861 describes the work as follows: "Jacob accompanies the flocks and other presents by the aid of which he hopes to appease the anger of his brother Esau. A stranger presents himself and engages with him in stubborn contest, which is terminated only at the moment when Jacob, touched on the tendon of his thigh by his adversary, finds himself reduced to impotence. This struggle is regarded by the Holy Books as a symbol of the tests that God sends sometimes to his elect."
6. For St. Michael as the angel in the story of Heliodorus, see e.g. Luce Laurand, *Saint-Michel et les Saints-Anges*, Paris, 1956, and also *Les Maccabées. Traduit en français avec une explication tirée des Saints-Pères...*, Paris, 1691, 334.
7. For an authoritative discussion of the Church's position in France at this time, see Dansette, *Histoire religieuse de la France*. He describes on

prematurely with Jacob "reduced to impotence," and not—as in the Bible—when the patriarch received the blessing and the name of Israel.[5]

The subject of Heliodorus may have seemed particularly attractive to the curé; for not only was it suited to the chapel (in its theme of angels guarding the temple, and in the angel rider who often was identified with St. Michael), but it could serve as a tribute to the Vatican.[6] Raphael's celebrated fresco (Fig. 70) had established the theme as a symbol of the Pope's victory over the Church's enemies, and by the late 1840's the papal (Ultramontane) party so dominated French Catholicism that even its opponents (the Gallicans) were compelled to seek its favor; furthermore, the French state in 1849, wishing the cooperation of the Church, as discussed in Chapter I, would gladly have subscribed to such a theme.[7] Whatever the reasons for the curé's acceptance of the subject, it is certain that Delacroix's motives had nothing to do with church politics and much to do with personal and artistic questions; for not only was the theme of painful punishment amid splendid luxury one which always interested him, but it was also the occasion for competition with the celebrated genius of Raphael.[8]

Several months after Delacroix finished the sketches for the three mural paintings, he wrote of them to Dutilleux: "You see me in these different subjects side by side with some great, quite imposing masters." Among these artists, the most important was undoubtedly Raphael, whose immense celebrity Delacroix may well have envied. Critics of the finished murals were to annoy him particularly when they placed the quality of Raphael's version of *Heliodorus* above his own. This spirit of rivalry must have intensified Delacroix's interest in the theme of one of the Renaissance master's most famous works, especially because copies (by Paul and Raymond

p. 332 how Mgr. Affre, Archbishop of Paris during the Revolution of 1848, achieved his position by accepting Ultramontane principles in order to win papal support, although he was a Gallican. It is remarkable that aside from one painting of Heliodorus—Antoine Richarte's in Valencia— only a few engravings of the theme were produced in France during the 18th century, according to A. Pigler, *Barockthemen*, Budapest and Berlin, 1956, I. Italy, on the other hand, produced eight or nine significant paintings of the theme in the 18th century. Countries other than Italy (Belgium, Austria) which used the theme also had Catholic hierarchies closely associated with Rome. I believe that the connection of the theme with the Pope and Roman Catholicism (discussed again below, Chapter IV)—traditional since Raphael—led the powerful Gallican hierarchy to reject it. Its re-emergence at Saint-Sulpice marks

the wane of Gallican influence, on the decline ever since the Concordat of 1801.

8. Baudelaire's famous poem for the 1867 version of the *Fleurs du Mal*, "Le Rebelle," which begins, "Un ange furieux fond du ciel comme un aigle," may have been composed with Delacroix's *Heliodorus* in mind, and reveals a similar sadism. The good angel—counterpart to the guardian angels of Heliodorus—punishes a sinner, while explaining the meaning of goodness to him. But the sinner replies, "I will not!" and the poem ends with the same intense punishment depicted in the painting. Dante, one of Delacroix's favorite authors, in referring to the story of Heliodorus, also emphasized the punishment, in *Purgatory*, Canto XX, 113: "We praise the hoof-kicks Heliodorus had...."

9. On the fame of the *Heliodorus*, cf., among many references, Fuseli, *Lectures*, Bonn, 1848, VIII: "The ultimate powers of Raphael...and of fresco

70 Raphael, *Heliodorus Driven from the Temple*. Rome, Vatican (photo: Alinari)

Balze), of Raphael's Stanze, including the *Heliodorus,* were continuously on view in the Pantheon in Paris from 1847 to 1873.[9] Delacroix saw the exhibition in February 1847, and became enthusiastic over these "reproductions of immortal masterpieces."

Raphael's greatness (like Michelangelo's) constantly tantalized Delacroix, who, while referring more than once to the earlier master's supreme abilities,[10] wished at the same time to set bounds to his greatness in order to find a place for other artists and other styles.[11] Delacroix was also aware of Ingres's devotion to Raphael, so that possibly in this instance the Romantic felt a double rivalry, with his contemporary unacknowledged in the background.[12]

In an article on Raphael, published when he was a little over thirty himself, Delacroix wrote: "Hardly thirty years old, Raphael, having attained perfection in the paintings of Siena, in the

appear to me collected in the...Heliodorus." On the Balze copies, see L. Flandrin, "Deux disciples d'Ingres. Paul et Raymond Balze," *GBA,* 4th ser., 6, 1911, 139-55, 317-32. The copy of the *Heliodorus* was executed in 1845 by Paul. For a history of the exhibition of the copies, see Flandrin, 330. Delacroix's letter was sent to M. Cavé on February 28 (1847) and is reprinted in the *Correspondance.* In it he praised the copies of the Stanze, defending them against the "pedants" who, having seen the originals, scorned the copies: "Les *loges* me paraissent particulièrement remarquables et respirer un entrain qu'on n'est pas accoutumé à rencontrer dans des répétitions. ..." Significantly, in the next paragraph the artist turned immediately to a discussion of work on his own murals in the Library of the Chamber of Deputies. Ingres, who had been the teacher of the Balze brothers, like Delacroix extolled the copies. (See Flandrin, 155.) Their common enthusiasm marks a striking point of contact between the tastes of these very different men. The main figure of Drolling's *Conversion of St. Paul* in a nearby chapel at Saint-Sulpice (completed as Delacroix was making his own first studies; see Appendix I, 1840), was possibly influenced by the Balze copy of *Heliodorus.*

10. E.g., *Journal,* I, 248, December 15, 1847: "All the great problems of art were solved in the 16th century. The perfection of drawing, of grace, of composition in Raphael." From the 18th century on (e.g. Reynolds), the geniuses of Raphael and of Michelangelo were opposed to one another. Delacroix painted not only a *Michelangelo in*

His Studio (1851), but a *Raphael in His Studio* (1831). Michelangelo's profound importance to the Romantic as a model of genius and art has often rightly been remarked. Delacroix himself wrote in his essay "On the Last Judgment," *Revue des deux mondes,* II, 1837: "Michelangelo is the father of modern art," a characteristic phrase, even though taken almost literally from Reynolds' Fifteenth Discourse. But for the paintings at Saint-Sulpice, his influence was negligible compared to that of Raphael. It is sometimes mistakenly stated that a medallion by Michelangelo in the Sistine Chapel treats the Heliodorus theme. See Grubar, "Two Drawings by Delacroix," and Louis Réau, *Iconographie de l'art chrétien,* Vol. II, *Iconographie de la bible,* Paris, 1956, pt. I, 307. The bronze medallion "The Death of Uriah," showing a fallen man attacked by a horseman and two men with sticks, is probably referred to. For an illustration, see Charles de Tolnay, *Michelangelo,* II (1945), 275, No. 223. De Tolnay lists nothing by Michelangelo concerning Heliodorus.

11. Cf. *Journal,* June 6, 1851: "Perhaps this exaltation that Raphael has in his lines, in the majority of his figures, Rembrandt has in the mysterious conception of his subject, in the profound naiveté of his expression and gestures. Although one could prefer this majestic emphasis of Raphael ...the great Dutchman was more naturally a painter than the studious pupil of Perugino."

12. The competition was made explicit when the recently finished decorations of the Hôtel de Ville by Ingres (1853) and by Delacroix (1854) were

School of Athens...."[13] The original manuscript, which is identical with the published version up to the list of Raphael's paintings, begins: "...*Heliodorus, School of Athens....*"[14] In the manuscript the word *Héliodore* is crossed out, and this painting, ranked first in the manuscript, is entirely omitted from the published article, giving the famous work an exceptional position and implying perhaps that it was not less but more important to him than those included in the list.[15] Two additional details show that Raphael was on the artist's mind at the beginning and end of his work on the project: not long after receiving his commission for the murals on February 11, 1850, Delacroix noted in his *Journal* "the fine project of going to Holland to see the drawings of Raphael"; and in his letter replying to Baudelaire, who had praised his paintings at Saint-Sulpice, he referred to the "arabesque" as an essential quality of his work. In this connection it is remarkable that the artist admired Raphael precisely for his "arabesque of line."[16] Thus, while many other influences affected the style and handling of his *Heliodorus*, one of the most important—especially in the choice of the theme—was the confrontation of Raphael's genius.

1. The Tradition of the Subjects

In his *Heliodorus*, Delacroix not only took up the challenge of Raphael's theme (as we have just seen), but carried several details from the Vatican fresco into his own painting: the reed whips of the angels, the rider's baton (which had been a spear in early sketches) and the horse's bridle (absent from early sketches). Possibly Delacroix was also influenced in his angel rider by engravings or an oil copy after another fresco in the Vatican attributed to Raphael (actually by G.

compared. See Sérullaz, *Les peintures*, 141-43, for the pertinent texts. A similar rivalry marked the Universal Exhibition of 1855, in which both artists had impressive entries. The Romantic was not at all indifferent to the *Ingriste* camp (not only because of its opposition to his membership in the Institute), nor to public opinion, and sometimes he actually covered up his spontaneous beginning when finishing a painting "in order to appear before the public." See the *Journal*, April 13, 1853. Delacroix's implicit criticism of the *Ingristes* has been discerned in his essay on Raphael (1830), among others by Christine Sieber-Meier, *Untersuchungen zum "Oeuvre Littéraire" von Eugène Delacroix*, Bern, 1963, 32; and in his essay, "Questions sur le beau" (1854) by Moreau-Nélaton, *Delacroix raconté*, II, 139-40.

13. Published in *Revue de Paris*, 1830, II.

14. Certainly known to Delacroix through Charles de Meulemeester's engravings of the Vatican frescoes from 1806 and later. See *Journal*, April 2, 1824. Another possible source might have been the well-known engravings of the frescoes by Volpis—also known as Volpato—and Morghen. Delacroix's original manuscript of the article is in the Institut d'Art et d'Archéologie, Paris. My quotation is from MS 250, Fol. 1, No. 36, p. 17.

15. Delacroix's touchiness about the similarity of his treatment to Raphael's led him, as we saw in the discussion of the evolution of the sketches, to make such changes as in Heliodorus' posture, which at first (Fig. 22) too closely resembled Raphael's corresponding figure. The relation seemed so obvious to Walter Pach that in his book *The Classical Tradition in Modern Art*, he simply juxtaposed reproductions (pls. 12 and 13) of Raphael's and Delacroix's versions, with the

Romano), *The Battle of the Milvian Bridge*.[17] In this fresco the mounted Constantine holds a spear aimed at enemies fallen beneath him, rides a bridled horse and has a posture similar to that of Delacroix's horseman. Such groups of horsemen over fallen enemies are frequent in French seventeenth century sculpture and painting, as in Coysevox's relief in the Salle Mars (de la Guerre) in Versailles, and especially in Lebrun's well-known battle pieces, which depend directly on Raphael.[18] (Lebrun's esteem among two generations of Romantics was such that Gros's *Battle of Aboukir* [1806] was compared to the *Battle of Arbela* of the Baroque master, by Girodet, and the artist himself was linked to David and Delacroix by Baudelaire as one of the giants of French painting.)[19]

Raphael's ingenious treatment of the biblical text in his *Heliodorus* was especially important for connecting the angel on horseback, the whipping angels and the prostrate Heliodorus. While this interpretation seems to render the text literally, in fact it unites three successive events. In the biblical account Heliodorus apparently was struck by the horse's hoofs and beaten with whips while standing. When he dropped to the ground, "thick darkness wrapped him round." Following Raphael, many artists, including Delacroix, combined the three successive moments into one image.[20] It has been shown that this interpretation, reflecting an incoherence in the text itself, brings together incompatible elements; *viz.*, the horse and rider theme of Greco-Roman origin, in which the enemy lies prostrate, and the flagellation theme of Jewish or Eastern origin, in which the victim stands.[21]

Although Delacroix adopted significant motifs from Raphael's painting, he treated the composition quite differently. This difference depends in part on the dissimilarity between the lower

comment (p. 40) that Delacroix "did not hesitate to invite comparison with Raphael."

16. Cf. Silvestre, *Les artistes français*, 19.

17. A copy in oil of Raphael's fresco, made by Bon Boulogne in the 17th century, was on view in the Louvre in 1854 and presumably earlier. See Frédéric Villot, *Notice des tableaux exposés dans les galéries du Musée Impérial du Louvre*, 1854, pt. I, 225, No. 392.

18. Lebrun copied Romano's *Battle of the Milvian Bridge* and used the horseman-over-fallen-enemy motif in several paintings. See the catalogue for the Lebrun Exhibition held at Versailles in 1963, Nos. 26, 30 and 31.

19. Girodet's *Critique des critiques du Salon de 1806* is discussed in Henry Lemonnier, *Gros*, Paris, n.d., 35, where it is pointed out that Girodet defended Gros's painting as having a different kind of poetry and truth from Lebrun's. Baudelaire's

remark, "Flanders has Rubens; Italy Raphael and Veronese; France has Lebrun, David and Delacroix," appeared in "Eugène Delacroix" (1863), and is published in *Mirror of Art*, 308. Delacroix was brought into closer contact with the Baroque artist when he decorated (as Lebrun was to have done) the ceiling of the Apollo Gallery of the Louvre. See the *Journal*, March 1850, passim, and Jennifer Montagu, "Le Brun et Delacroix dans la galerie d'Apollon," *La revue du Louvre et des musées de France*, 5, 1962, 233-36.

20. Delacroix may have studied Raphael's *Heliodorus*, not only from the Balze copies or from engravings (as already mentioned above), but from such books as John Burnet's *Education of the Eye*, published in 1837, with a discussion and illustration of the fresco.

21. See Elias Bikerman, "Héliodore au Temple de Jérusalem," in *Annuaire de l'Institut de Philolo-*

edges of the frame—straight in the one case, crooked in the other;[22] but Raphael's solutions differ significantly even in paintings with similarly crooked lower edges, such as the *Mass of Bolsena* and the *Delivery of St. Peter,* which are superbly balanced compositions with a quiet lucidity far from the dramatic emphases of light and mass in Delacroix's painting. While Raphael divided his composition of the *Heliodorus* into three equal parts, arranged so that the two sides balance about an empty center, Delacroix divided his unevenly, placing the Heliodorus group near the center foreground. Reconciling with apparent ease the picture surface with its depth, the Renaissance artist projected an ample and legible space in which a gently pervasive rhythm connects the three separate regions, and in which a precise and consistent foreshortening clarifies the position and size of all the forms. That the romantic artist, who understood perspective,[23] preferred not to use it is clear from a comparison of details in the two versions, such as the rider's baton: in the one it is neatly foreshortened, whereas in the other it is turned parallel to the picture plane (like the soldier's spear), to avoid foreshortenings. Raphael's smooth, elegant architecture, nearly devoid of ornament, his broad, flat ground without a dais, and the gestures and garb of his figures have no counterpart in Delacroix's version; indeed this brilliant solution to the specific problem of integrating the papal cortège and a biblical miracle, while generally admired and often engraved, was rarely adopted by later artists.[24]

gie et d'Histoire orientale et slave, 1944, VII, 5-40. Professor Bikerman, after proving that the inconsistency in the paintings of Raphael and Delacroix corresponds to an incoherence in the text, demonstrates that the passage in Maccabees is a compound of two different texts. Professor Schapiro first called my attention to this article.

22. The lower edge of Delacroix's painting is cut into by the door to the Chapelle du Péristyle in the south tower.

23. RF 10, 147r (Fig. 64), one of the sketches for the *Heliodorus,* has, as we have seen, studies of perspective.

24. Some artists split the composition (C. Rancini engraved the right half) and others excerpted one or two figures (Bouchardon's engraving). Especially in the north, artists from the 16th century on made the punishment the central action, giving Onias little space, often placing him to the side as the shocked witness of the event, with arms spread in astonishment. The representation of Onias reached its nadir in a French 17th century Bible, in which the priest is mingled with a crowd in the remote background behind the chastized Heliodorus, while two conversing sol-

diers fill the foreground as repoussoir figures. The legend below reads: "Heliodorus, wishing to rob the temple treasury, is thrown down by an armed horseman." Above, the homely moral, which has left far behind Raphael's parable of God saving the Church in answer to the Pope's prayer, reads (in Latin): "Do not desire what you are not allowed to have." The Cabinet des Estampes, B.N., which owns this engraving, has several others of the theme by the following artists: B. Salomon, 16th century; E. Hoes, 16th century; Callot (?); Chauveau (?), 1680. While not adhering to Raphael's composition, French 17th century engravers, both in their details and in their precise manner of drawing, basically continue Raphael's treatment of the subject. With the new sensuous art and the painterly style prevalent in 18th century France, we should expect some interesting translations of the 17th century engravers' work by the painters; however, during this period in France the subject is rarely treated, and we must look to Italy for versions in the 18th century. Solimena's painting in the church of Gesù Nuovo at Naples shows how far even Italian versions of the theme have moved in the 18th century from Raphael's; it is

Paradoxically, Delacroix's dynamic painting in certain details is more closely tied to its frame than Raphael's; e.g., the two central columns in the painting rise almost directly above the outer edges of the door-jambs, and a series of stepped forms (the dais, the staircase) repeat the irregular lower edge. Delacroix's straight columns and steps produce an effect almost of a theater curtain from which the more painterly figures seem detached, providing a tension not felt in Raphael's painting, where the sculpturesque figures fit the architecture. These distinctions between the two paintings mark the great differences between the styles and personalities of their artists. It is clear that Raphael's influence alone cannot account for the rectilinearity of Delacroix's painting, which disappointed some connoisseurs of an artist who favored curving lines and arabesques in opposition to the stringent line of the *Ingristes*.

The placement of dramatically moving figures and curved lines against a comparatively straight-lined architecture suggests the Neoclassical followers of Poussin and Lebrun. In their work classic balance degenerated into inertness, as in the decorations of the chapels neighboring Delacroix's at Saint-Sulpice, which hardly affected his own solution, and in the painting of his teacher P.-N. Guérin (1774-1833).[25] Guérin adopted austere architectural backgrounds for his figures in the French theatrical tradition, and sent his pupils to the theater to study gesture and

full of minor actions lacking both the clarity and the relative conciseness of the Renaissance fresco.

25. David's most characteristic work, such as the *Oath of the Horatii*, places dramatic figures in the foreground against a stately architecture. His carefully planned staging, with its balanced gestures and movements, is rooted in the same impulse toward a classicist equilibrium found already in the art of Poussin and E. Lesueur. While Delacroix departed considerably from the methods and style of David, he did not feel—as claimed by George P. Mras, *Eugène Delacroix's Theory of Art*, Princeton, 1966, 64, 71—"a general hostility to David" or that David was a "sterile classicist." Cf. Delacroix's article on Prudhon, *Revue des deux mondes*, November 1, 1846 (cited in note 45 below), for his favorable opinions of David. For a discussion of the relation between Delacroix's stagelike effects in certain paintings and Poussin's, see the important article by Klaus Berger, "Poussin's Style in the 19th Century," *GBA*, 6th ser., 46, 1955, 161-71. Two of the better known among the artists decorating chapels at Saint-Sulpice were the Davidians A. Vinchon and Abel de Pujol. The former, in his *St. Maurice ... Refusing to Sacrifice to False Gods* (1821), arranged his

figures on a platform with four steps leading up to it and set his entire foreground group in a setting of classical architecture. The result is not impressive, for Vinchon failed to integrate figures and setting, and did not unify his surface, so that the steps jut out conspicuously, whereas the temple is lost in shadow. Abel de Pujol decorated the Chapelle de Saint-Roch in 1822 with two paintings using architecture as a background. *St. Roch Healing the Plague-Stricken* shows steps and a balcony with figures, composed very differently from the *Heliodorus* in having an empty space in the foreground, with middleground figures grouped on a low balcony. The bearded sick man at the left with his left arm over his head is very similar to the soldier in the right foreground of the *Heliodorus*, especially in early sketches. In Pujol's other painting, *The Death of St. Roch*, there appear small figures walking down steps in the background in sharp contrast to several large foreground figures, a motif also used by David and probably derived from Fontainebleau. In his *Journal* on February 4, 1850, Delacroix actually mentioned Pujol's nearby chapel in connection with his own; but these paintings—like the other attenuated Davidian compositions in neighbor-

physiognomy.[26] His linear severity seems to have provoked the young Delacroix—who worked in his studio in 1816—to a conscious rebellion against straight lines; nevertheless, in certain paintings just this linearity can be felt, as in the architectural background of the *Taking of Constantinople* of 1840 (Louvre), a painting of which the artist made a second version in 1852 (Louvre), and in the architecture of the *Trajan* of 1840 (Louvre), on both of whose backgrounds Boulangé collaborated.[27] The style of his helpers Andrieu and Boulangé, who collaborated on the background of the *Heliodorus* and who were less inspired than the master, may have contributed to its stiffness, thus sharpening the contrast with the figures before it.[28] But Delacroix himself chose to emphasize the architectural aspect of the subject, mainly, I believe, in order to balance the curving lines of the *Jacob*. However, while stiff compared to the animated backgrounds he usually painted, the architecture has some lively passages and dramatic lighting effects (to be discussed presently).

The dramatic concentration and virtuoso handling of parts of the *Heliodorus* bring to mind Delacroix's relation to Rubens, who was the master most often studied by him, for instance in connection with the mural decorations of the library of the Palais Bourbon.[29] Rubens was a favorite of the early Romantics who, like their predecessors, the heroic and serious Davidians, turned against what they regarded as the effeminacy and inanity of eighteenth century art, preferring the healthy exuberance of the Baroque master to the sensual excesses of Boucher. While after the late 1830's a vogue—especially in the minor arts—for the eighteenth century gradually overcame this earlier contempt, except among older Davidian critics,[30] Delacroix himself wrote in his *Journal* as late as September 13, 1857 that everything following Lebrun and "above all the whole eighteenth century is nothing but banality and routine." Still, some students of Dela-

ing chapels—seem only slightly to have affected his composition of the *Heliodorus*.

26. See Benoit, *L'art français*.

27. *The Taking of Constantinople* resembles Guérin's *Aeneas Recounting to Dido the Misfortunes of Troy* (Louvre) in some details: the columns supporting an entablature, the entire spatial composition and the distant coastline passing behind the columns. On Boulangé, see the general Introduction, and the introduction to Chapter II. On his painting the backgrounds of the *Trajan* and of *The Taking of Constantinople*, see Joubin's note in the *Journal*, III, 533, citing a letter of Burty.

28. For a discussion of the role of the helpers, see the general Introduction and the introduction to Chapter II. The precise contributions of the helpers are difficult to determine.

29. See e.g. his remark to his pupil Louis de Planet, cited in De Planet's *Souvenirs*, 38: "When one paints, he should have beside him some studies of Rubens, in order to be able to consult them, above all for the tones...." Delacroix's murals in the library of the Palais Bourbon were painted with De Planet.

30. See Seymour O. Simches, *Le romantisme et le goût esthétique du XVIIIe siècle*, Paris, 1964, 36, for the criticism of this taste by Delécluze, the Davidian critic of Delacroix, and passim for its revival. The older view that the revival of interest in the 18th century began, rather than merely culminated, with the Goncourt brothers is maintained by Meier-Graefe in *Eugène Delacroix*, 55.

31. See Ernest Chesneau's comments published in the introduction to the Robaut Catalogue, xl, and Meier-Graefe's remarks, *Eugène Delacroix*, 55.

croix have observed a connection between his painting and that of the century he maligned. Chesneau remarked that the Romantic's art was a transformation of the eighteenth century's elegant grace into imposing and majestic terms, and Meier-Graefe asserted that Delacroix, while actually admiring Watteau and the eighteenth century, "drank at the sources" and went back to Raphael and Rubens.[31] I might add that to some extent Delacroix must have seen and interpreted these "sources" through the accumulated experiences and perceptions of the century between.[32]

Whereas Raphael's influence on Delacroix's *Heliodorus* is demonstrable both for the theme and in details, Rubens' is subtler and has more to do with the general qualities of composition and handling. The distinction between these influences, the one based on emulation, the other on affinity, is clearly visible in the angel rider, a figure treated at first like a warrior or like a huntsman with a spear, suggesting Rubens' animated figures, and only gradually and by the necessities of composition transformed into a serene, more Raphaelesque angel with a baton. Even in the finished version the whirling group of Heliodorus and the angels is reminiscent of similar groups in Rubens' military and hunting scenes so well known to Delacroix through engravings.[33] Characteristically, the artist took particular interest in Rubens while composing his sketches for the concurrent projects in Saint-Sulpice and in the Louvre, and probably studied engravings of the Flemish master's painting as an inspiration for his own.[34] I am especially reminded of the dramatic movement of figures and drapery in Rubens' *Mystic Marriage of St. Catherine* (1627-1628) over the altar of the church of Saint Augustine in Antwerp, which Delacroix saw in 1850, but which he knew from an engraving he owned, and which he admired long before beginning work on the *Heliodorus*.[35]

32. All the important issues that engaged Delacroix's epoch were inherited from the late 18th century, which crystallized earlier thought: studio painting vs. painting out-of-doors, line vs. color and mass, expression vs. correctness, *"le beau idéal"* vs. *"le vrai idéal,"* and Gros's insistence, against the academy of his day, on Rubens as the best guide for artists. On these issues see Benoit, *L'art français*, passim.

33. On the sketches see above, Chapter II. On Rubens, De Planet, *Souvenirs*, has much to say; also see *Journal*, January 24, 1847: "The influence of the principal lines is immense in a composition, I have under my eyes the *Hunts* of Rubens; one among others, the *Lion Hunt*, engraved by Soutman...." In 1849, several months before he fixed his subjects for the chapel, he copied at the Louvre Rubens' *Embarkation of Maria de' Medici*. Lassalle-Bordes pointed out the importance to Delacroix of engravings in his letter to Burty, n.d., MS 245, Institut d'Art et d'Archéologie, Paris, p. 15: "He composed his paintings with extreme facility; but beforehand he leafed through his boxes containing many engravings of different schools...," then he "...transformed his borrowings (*larcins*) to the point of making them unrecognizable."

34. Delacroix felt that his study of Rubens' *Elevation of the Cross* at Antwerp would aid him in working out his composition for the Apollo ceiling, although the subjects had nothing in common. See *Journal*, August 10, 1850.

35. When he visited Antwerp, he made an entry in his *Journal* dated July 8, 1850: "I had been to St. Augustine before. Great painting of Rubens on the altar, and made for the place. *Mystic Marriage of St. Catherine*. Superb composition for which I have the engraving."

Important features of the two paintings broadly agree with one another: the general proportions and vertical axes; the column before which a prominent drapery blows (to the left in Rubens', to the right in Delacroix's); the steps with figures leading up to a dais;[36] and the varied and highly demonstrative gestures of some figures, which point or turn or spread out their arms in wonder or awe.

Of the many differences in detail between the two paintings, one which must be accounted for is the presence of a balcony with the Onias group looking down.[37] In this Delacroix differs also from Raphael, whose devoutly isolated Onias was situated only one step above Heliodorus. To the post-Raphaelite conception of Onias as an active participant, Delacroix has added a high balcony for him and his witnessing congregation to stand on.

Such arrangements of figures on a balcony are found above all in Venetian painting from before Veronese's *Wedding at Cana* to after Tiepolo's *Banquet of Cleopatra*. Tintoretto's *St. Mark*, which may very well have suggested (as some contemporary critics thought) the angel at the right who sweeps down on Heliodorus, has two figures on a low balcony to the left.[38] Delacroix could have studied the arrangement either in the Louvre *Wedding at Cana* or in such eighteenth century Gobelin tapestries as *Mary Magdalen in the Home of the Pharisee*. The romantic artist's interest in Venetian balconies went back at least to 1826, when he painted the *Execution of Marino Faliero* (Robaut No. 160),[39] and his solution essentially combines one of these balconies with the big central column and dais of Rubens.

36. The idea of placing figures on the steps is not unique to Rubens, of course, but it may have been brought more forcefully to his attention by contact with the *Mystic Marriage*, either through direct study of it, or through his reading of Reynolds, whose works were translated into French in 1806, and who remarked, with regard to Rubens' altarpiece, which he discussed at length and with admiration in "A Journey to Flanders and Holland," *Works*, London, 1798 (3 vols.), II, 309: "By way of link to unite the upper and lower part of the picture, are four female saints half-way up the steps...." At this time Delacroix often used steps to unify the space vertically, e.g. in the *Resurrection of Lazarus* (1850) and the *Pilgrims of Emmaus* (1851-52).

37. Balconies with figures appear in some of Rubens' paintings, e.g. the Brussels *Adoration of the Magi* and the *Conversion of St. Bavo* in Ghent. In 1841 Delacroix copied Rubens' *The Miracle of St. Benedict* (1628), Brussels, a painting with figures on a balconied landing above steps. For an illustration of Delacroix's copy, also in Brussels, see pl. 2 of the catalogue of the Delacroix Exhibition held in Bordeaux in 1963.

38. The painting was seen by Delacroix in the Musée Napoléon, according to Silvestre, *Les artistes français*, 24.

39. Delacroix, who never visited Italy, based the architecture of the doge's palace and much of his composition on *The Palace of the Doges*, painted in 1826 by his friend the artist Richard Parkes Bonington, who had visited Venice that year. Traces of Bonington's earlier influence crop up continually in Delacroix's mature work.

40. The composition with two large figures dates back to the 5th century parchment miniature of the Vienna Genesis. For illustrations see J.-D. Stefanescu, *Iconographie de la Bible*, Paris, 1938, No. 22. T. Ehrenstein, *Das Alte Testament im Bilde*, Vienna, 1923, lists illustrations for the 12th and 13th centuries. A discussion of later illustrations of the story can be found in Mrs. Jameson's

In illustrating *Jacob Wrestling with the Angel*, Delacroix faced a different problem in the setting. Two treatments of the theme—as an incident in the life of Jacob, and as a landscape—generally remained distinct up to the seventeenth century, and to each way corresponds a different conception of the composition: as part of a series of episodes from Jacob's life, two large figures in the foreground fill the greater part of the picture space, with or without an accompaniment of landscape and caravan details;[40] as part of a landscape, the two wrestling figures are generally lost in an encompassing forest.[41]

Delacroix's version seems to fit neither tradition: the landscape—remote from the classic approach of Raphael or Poussin—is large and vigorous, and at the same time the figures are seen close up and by no means lost in the landscape; in short, it successfully combines a drama in the foreground in the manner of history painting with a rich and extensive landscape.[42] This achievement brings the *Jacob* into relation with an antecedent universally admired as the ideal example of such a combination, and whose fame rivaled that of Raphael's *Heliodorus*—Titian's *Death of St. Peter the Martyr* (Fig. 71). This painting, regarded by many as the culmination of Titian's powers, was often engraved and copied, and was called by Constable "the foundation of all the styles of landscape" (in the seventeenth century), a remark later echoed by Delacroix, who called Titian the "creator of landscape."[43] In England many of the Royal Academy lectures discussed it, and Turner based a painting on its composition. In France, after Napoleon I had seized the painting from Italy, it became a model for landscape until its destruction by fire in

The History of Our Lord, 2nd ed., London, 1861, 2 vols.

41. An illustration of two small figures in a large landscape at the Cabinet des Estampes is from the 17th century (after P. Brill?). Cf. also Claude's painting in the Hermitage, *Jacob Wrestling with the Angel* (1672; also called "Night"). As is often true of Claude's figures, the wrestlers are swallowed up in the large landscape setting.

42. Raphael's Vatican fresco, the *Parnassus*, has a characteristic landscape composed within a comfortable space and in a gracefully structural style; the vertical, straight trees define planes parallel to the picture plane. A similar quality of classical ordering pervades the work of Poussin, of whom Delacroix wrote in his *Journal* on September 19, 1847: "His landscapes have something too arranged about them." E. Lesueur, although influenced by Poussin, was more of a colorist, better able to unify his painting, and preferred by Delacroix on that account, according to the *Journal* entry on June 6, 1851. Certain very gen-

eral parallels can be found between paintings in Lesueur's Hôtel Lambert series of the life of St. Bruno (retouched by Delacroix in 1844), and the *Jacob*, but after Lesueur, little in French classicism reminds one of the mural decoration. With the Neoclassic Davidians, indeed, the core of monumentality in French classic landscape was turned inside out: architecture almost completely displaced landscape as a background.

43. Constable's remark is included among his notes on six lectures on landscape, delivered in June 1833, and published in C. R. Leslie, *Memoirs of the Life of John Constable*, R.A., ed. Benedict Nicolson, London, 1949, 312. Delacroix's statement appears in the *Journal*, January 1, 1857. Delacroix knew and admired Leslie, but a more demonstrable source for his opinions is John Burnet, *Practical Hints on Colour in Painting*, which Delacroix read. (This work was published in several editions during the first half of the 19th century: 1st ed., London, 1827; 5th ed., London, 1843.) See the Supplement to the *Journal*,

1867.[44] Delacroix not only saw the painting, but owned the oil copy Géricault painted after the original, and which the latter prized above most of his forty copies after other masters.[45]

A similarity between the landscapes of the two paintings had been pointed out already by Gautier in 1861.[46] Titian's painting depicts a murder among relatively large figures in the foreground, set against a landscape whose big trees extend up toward the arched frame and cross each other at several places, as though echoing the interlocking action below. The whole arrangement of Titian's painting probably suggested the basic compositional idea of the *Jacob*, as is clear from early sketches in which the trees intertwine much like Titian's. On the other hand, in the finished version the trees are relatively straight and vertical, suggesting that the artist consciously departed from his model—as he had done for the *Heliodorus*—when he evolved his composition. Other equally significant differences distinguish the composition of the *St. Peter Martyr* from that of the *Jacob*: the foliage of its trees starts higher than the *Jacob's*; its lower and more even ground does not frame the figures, so that a large proportion of the painting contains sky; its treetops part near the frame to make room for flying putti; and its space recedes in a series of classical parallel planes from the three foreground figures to the distant trees.

The differences between Titian and Delacroix correspond to those between Raphael and the Romantic, and point once more toward the Baroque dynamism of Rubens. Significantly, Delacroix linked the two artists in his *Journal:* "Nothing equals the landscapes of Titian and of Rubens. Those of the latter are the most admirable for imagination."[47] It is hard to isolate any single work of Rubens as a source for the *Jacob;* but the Flemish master's dynamic hunting scenes, often studied and copied both from originals and from engravings, or paintings with

III, 380, n.d., which quotes—without reference—from the discussion of pl. VI in the French ed. of 1835. The importance of this work to Delacroix has recently been emphasized by Lee Johnson, *Delacroix*, London, 1963. I believe that the most important aspect of Burnet's writing is his transmission of Reynolds' ideas to the 19th century, bringing them up to date and adding examples. Sieber-Meier, *Untersuchungen*, discusses Reynolds' *Discourses* as a source for Delacroix's writings in art criticism.

44. For some of the Royal Academy lectures extolling the work, see: Reynolds' Discourse XI; Opie's Lecture IV, 1807; and Fuseli's *Lectures*, 452. Turner's painting based on Titian's is his *Adonis Parting for the Chase*, 1806-10, Gallery of Modern Art, New York.

45. Géricault's copy, one of ten such copies owned by Delacroix, was No. 234 in the Vente Delacroix of 1864, and is listed as No. 179 in Charles

Clément, *Géricault*, 320. On its value to Géricault, see Clément, 264. Although Delacroix knew the painting both in the original and in engravings, this copy—which I have unfortunately been unable to locate—may have had particular importance for its colors and brushwork. Titian's painting was on exhibit in the Musée Napoléon, where Delacroix probably saw it in his youth. See the *Journal*, October 20, 1853, and Delacroix's article "Prudhon," *Revue des deux mondes*, November 1, 1846, reprinted in *Oeuvres littéraires*, II, *Essais sur les artistes célèbres*, Paris, 1923, ed. E. Faure, 132. Delacroix cites great works gathered in the Luxembourg Museum, including Titian's *Peter Martyr* and Tintoretto's *Saint Mark*. Also, cf. Silvestre, *Les artistes français*, 24.

46. See below, Chapter IV and the Appendix of criticism (III).

47. See the *Journal*, Supplement, III, 367, ca. 1840.

71 Titian, *Death of St. Peter the Martyr*, engraving by Martino Rota, London, Courtauld Institute of Art
(photo: Witt Library)

interlocked figures in a landscape like the *Kermesse* in the Louvre, may have given Delacroix hints for the broad movements of his composition and for the animation of his figures, especially in the caravan.[48]

Earlier art can only in part account for Delacroix's conception of the *Jacob*, for the joint project of the *Heliodorus* must also have affected its composition. It is worth noting at this point that the artist's own easel paintings affected or were affected by the murals; e.g. the *Lion and Cayman* of 1855 (Louvre), which is very close to the *Jacob* in its landscape setting, its arrangement of forms and above all in its coloring and tonality. The relationship of the easel and mural paintings has recently been investigated for the earlier period of the Palais Bourbon in an admirable unpublished dissertation.[49] There are, to be sure, significant differences between the two murals, corresponding to their different subjects: the vertical-horizontal lines of the architecture as against the tilted ones of the landscape; the smooth surfaces and lines of the temple painted in muted grays and yellows as against the rough-grained barks of the trees and the curving lines of the earth and the foliage painted in vivid greens; and the relatively near, closed walls of the temple as against the deep vista in the landscape, extending on the left to the sky. Yet we know that Delacroix conceived the paintings in the same period, and one sketch shows studies for the two paintings together. Aside from some details of the figures (e.g. the face of the angel on horseback and of the angel wrestling with Jacob, and their wings) the paintings broadly resemble one another in their compositions. The main action in both paintings occurs between figures of similar size placed in the foreground as on a stage; in each painting there are forms which enclose the main actors as in a curtain: the foliage of the trees and the walls of the temple, and the three large trees are arranged in a straight row which recedes diagonally at the same angle and to the same depth as the two columns of the temple.

48. Delacroix told his friend C. Dutilleux that every time he went to Champrosay he took with him some engravings after Rubens' work. See Robaut, No. 1732. A characteristic oil copy, probably done in the mid-1840's, is of Rubens' *Boar Hunt* (Dresden), which depicts a scramble of men and beasts in a wooded landscape setting. My belief that Delacroix's copy, now in Munich, dates perhaps as late as 1849 has been strengthened by the opinion of Dr. Siegfried Wichmann, Conservator of the Bayerische Staatsgemäldesammlungen, expressed in a letter to me dated September 4, 1962. Unfortunately, I am not certain of the provenance of Rubens' painting during this time. There are several resemblances between the *Boar Hunt* and the *Jacob*: the diagonal movement from the lower right to the upper left; the pair of thick trees diverging from a common base and forming an isosceles triangle with inverted vortex; the dog in the lower right which, like Jacob's spear, points toward the main action; the high ground in the center with the clearings on either side through which the sky is visible (a Flemish rather than an Italian convention); and the horse in the lower right corner. The differences between Delacroix's copy of the hunt scene and his mural in shape, color and scale of the figures are not less important than the similarities, and parallels could have been found in other paintings of the Flemish master known to the Romantic. The influence, as already pointed out, was in the spirit rather than the detail.

49. See Robert N. Beetem, "Delacroix's Mural Paintings, 1833-47," doctoral dissertation, University

The composition of the *St. Michael* is the least successful of the three paintings. Delacroix himself (in a letter to Dutilleux dated October 5, 1850) seems not to have considered it as important as the *Heliodorus* or the *Jacob*, nor does it rank in achievement with his two other ceiling decorations of this period, the one in the Louvre, the other in the Hôtel de Ville (to judge the latter from surviving sketches). The ceiling occupies a most unfortunate position with respect to the chapel lighting, so that whereas its greater distance from the spectator necessitates more light than the two other murals, it actually receives less from the window due to its height. Those who have discussed the murals have had least to say about it, and I will also make my discussion brief.[50]

I feel that the main difficulty of the *St. Michael* lies in the formal ambiguity of its composition: neither axis of the ellipse clearly dominates.[51] On the other hand, the archangel's vertical thrust with his spear along the minor axis of the ellipse is too strong to permit a circular movement (along the circling cloud forms and the bodies on the ground) to dominate. As was shown in the discussion of the sketches, Delacroix projected two solutions to his composition which were opposed, and between which he wavered, so that his cogent ideas were not realized in the ceiling itself.

The history of the familiar subject of St. Michael extends through countless paintings, including the famous versions of Raphael (attributed), Guido Reni and Domenichino. During the sixteenth century the theme became, like that of Heliodorus, a widespread symbol of the Church's victory over its enemies.[52] That the enemy, the Devil, was given attributes which became increasingly less monstrous and more human after the sixteenth century marks the triumph of the humanistic viewpoint. The theme of a bestial man like Lucifer being speared by his conqueror might seem particularly suited to Delacroix's temperament, but actually in this case it was not,

of California, Berkeley, 1964, Dissertation Abstracts No. 65-2947.

50. A further difficulty in making a detailed study of the ceiling arises from its having been restored. Even before the ceiling was finished, at least the ornamental, garlanded frame had been damaged by humidity and restored (as mentioned already), according to the *Journal*, April 10, 1860. More serious damage seems to have occurred later, to judge from the "Rapport de l'Architecte de la 5e section, Préfet du Département de la Seine, No. 2080, Paris, Dec. 21, 1891," in *Archives de la Seine*, V 71 M³² 2, which states that "A repair of the painting decorating the ceiling of the Chapelle des Saints-Anges, occasioned by an infiltration of water, was being made...."

51. Even 18th century oval paintings, as of Boucher or Fragonard, reveal one main axis as dominant —generally the long axis—with the painting arranged so that verticality coincides with the long axis. Watteau also often makes the long axis vertical, but in his *Jupiter and Antiope* (Louvre), he shows a less frequent use of it as horizontal. Delacroix's difficulties with the composition may also have resulted from his irresolution whether to foreshorten the major figures, as in his first version, or to place them parallel to the picture plane, as in his final version, which in this regard resembles the two other murals.

52. See e.g. *L'Apocalypse de Saint-Jean, traduit en français avec l'explication du sens littéral...par Sr. Le Maistre de Sacy Prêtre*, Brussels, 1703, 173, comment on the Apocalypse of St. John, Rev. 12:7-13: "...we remark in the Scripture examples of this continual combat of good and bad angels, in which we see that St. Michael was the de-

perhaps because the archangel, an infinitely powerful agent, stood for something complacently superior; consequently, the artist could not show St. Michael as feeling sadistic pleasure or disgust toward the Devil. Not unnaturally, the Romantic's most fascinating figures are villains like Lucifer and the lesser demons crawling along the edges of the ceiling decoration. In the *Heliodorus,* for similar reasons, the angel rider succeeds less than the secondary figures of the whippers.

Delacroix's interpretation combines the traditional combat of angels with a clash of light and shadow as in his concurrent project for the ceiling of the Apollo Gallery. Here, one senses a closeness to eighteenth century art with its plays of lights and darks, which we find in some landscape idylls of Fragonard and Boucher. As already mentioned, Lemoyne's oval ceiling for the Chapel of the Virgin at Saint-Sulpice probably helped determine the first version of the *St. Michael.* Lemoyne's painting, finished in 1732, shows the Virgin in the center of cloud-borne adoring saints, and the light is, as in Delacroix's first version, darker along the edges and irregularly spotted over the painting. At a very early phase of his project, as discussed in Chapter II, Delacroix had occasion to study Lemoyne's painting closely.

From this brief analysis, I conclude that the *St. Michael* is as difficult to appreciate as to study. While some figures, especially among the fallen angels, are masterfully painted, they are lost in shadows and all but invisible to spectators. Among the factors contributing to the weakness of the painting may have been the artist's poor health and advancing years, which induced him, e.g., to give up the idea of retouching the frames at one point. The high ceiling would have posed difficulties even to a stronger and younger man, so that a large part of the less accessible upper regions was probably finished and retouched by helpers, especially Andrieu. There seems, in fact, to be a gradient of quality, with the best work below, even in the lower paintings.[53] Consequently the *St. Michael* made less impact on Delacroix's contemporaries than the powerful paintings of the *Heliodorus* and the *Jacob.*

The four pendentives in grisaille below *St. Michael* (as well as the frames) are subordinate to the large paintings thematically and stylistically. Each is filled with an angel who, like the putti of the Salon du Roi, holds an emblem: a harp, a torch, a censer, and a book (see Figs. 68 and 69). Although for each of these attributes one could find a symbol associated with guardian

fender of the Synagogue—Dan. 10.13, c. 12.21—as he now is of the Church." The significance of the choice of this theme for the relations of the contemporary Church and State is discussed above in the general Introduction and in Chapter I, and below in Chapter IV.

53. I definitely do not mean—as some of Delacroix's contemporary critics claimed—that his artistic capacity declined, but only his physical ability.

54. The evidence is not conclusive, and either or both helpers may have worked on the pendentives: Delacroix wrote a letter to Boulangé on

May 14, 1860, directing his work on the grisailles; but Andrieu owned a sheet with nine sketches of the pendentive angels, listed as No. 1338 in Robaut, suggesting that he worked on them.

55. For Delacroix's use of the word *enfant* see J. J. Guiffrey, "Le Salon du Roi...Peintures décoratives d'Eugène Delacroix décrites par l'artiste," *L'art,* 2, 1878, 257-68.

56. A memo of Baltard for the year 1856 mentions that "the four pendentives were fired and scraped to the bottom" that year.

57. See Louis Vitet, "La Chapelle des Saints-Anges

angels, it is clear that Delacroix himself viewed the pendentives as ornamental adjuncts of the paintings, and he left the execution of the grisailles largely up to the helpers working under his supervision.[54] In calling his figures "children," the artist showed that he considered the angels as decoration rather than as devotional images; for he used the same word for the similar figures of putti bordering the main paintings on the ceiling of the Salon du Roi, who carry the emblems of such pagan deities as Minerva and Mercury.[55] Delacroix chose his final subjects for the pendentives from a list he made up as late as August 14, 1851, long after finishing his sketches for the three big paintings, and their final execution was not begun before 1856.[56] If the artist intended the grisaille repeated at four key points to unify the chapel, as a contemporary critic thought they did, and to bring out the three bigger paintings by their comparative brightness, then one wonders why he used so strong a gold for the frame of the *St. Michael*, thereby cutting the grisailles off from the ceiling.[57] Actually, this may not have seemed a serious difficulty to Delacroix, who regarded the architecture primarily as support and protection for the paintings, and who believed that gold ornamentation is best for oil paintings (having used it regularly in his earlier mural decorations).[58] Perhaps the artist, aware of the many impressive gilt decorations at Versailles and in the Louvre, merely considered gold frames as the most fitting accompaniment of great painting.

2. Biblical Authenticity, Exoticism and Romantic Realism

As pointed out in the Introduction Delacroix originally conceived his paintings in the midst of a revival of taste for both Greek and Jewish antiquity. The convincing "biblical" details of the chapel decorations impressed many of his contemporaries, the *Heliodorus* particularly interesting them for its novel representation of the Temple of Jerusalem. French classicists, both in the theater and in painting, had long preoccupied themselves with this problem, and writers had for centuries speculated inconclusively about it. Delacroix was well aware of the uncertainties with regard to reconstructions of the Temple when he wrote: "There remains for us nothing of the architecture or of the arts of the Hebrews, but one must not suppose that their works were inferior to those of the neighboring nations, with whom they had continual relations. The Holy Books speak in magnificent terms of the Temple of Jerusalem...."[59] Although the nineteenth

à Saint-Sulpice...," *Revue des deux mondes*, 38, 1862, 713, which praises the four angels in grisaille "so calm, so modest, so soberly placed to unite...by neutral tones the brilliant light of the side walls to that of the ceiling."

58. Delacroix quoted Chevreul on gilt frames as best for oil paintings in his notebook for the scientist's lectures in January 1848, preserved in the Cabinet des Dessins, Louvre. The artist had already considered gold ornamentation even before receiving his final commission for the chapel. See *Journal*, March 2, 1849. Cf. Moreau-Nélaton,

Eugène Delacroix, II, 85, which discusses a letter to Soulier dated September 6, 1827: "'J'ai achevé le tableau d'animaux du général et je lui ai déterré un cadre rococo, que je fais redorer, et qui fera merveille....' Le cadre 'rococo' déterré par Delacroix pour habiller son oeuvre et redoré par ses soins, n'est autre qu'une de ces bordures en bois sculpté de style Louis XIV dont le goût du temps faisant fi...."

59. In "Des variations du beau," published in *Revue des deux mondes*, 10, 1857.

century knew little more than the preceding centuries about the actual appearance of ancient architecture, including the Temple of Jerusalem, a new image had emerged through the publishing of a series of biblical explorations. From the sixteenth to the eighteenth century, the classicized model of biblical architecture was gradually expanded to include references to the findings of Oriental archaeologists. Even the definition of classical architecture itself, once restricted to a small group of Roman and Greek monuments, could at last admit examples from the Orient.[60]

These changes of viewpoint help to explain why Delacroix's architecture, while in part dependent upon a classical tradition (we have seen—besides the stimulation of classic stage design—how his very choice of subject vies with Raphael's *Heliodorus*), nevertheless departs considerably from it. Major differences in scale and decoration are apparent between the architecture depicted by the Neoclassicist Guérin and by Delacroix. The Romantic's architecture is grandiose compared to older architectural settings, and his walls, unlike the bare walls of French classical representations from Poussin to Guérin, are lavishly ornamented. Even the straight line of Delacroix's temple, already discussed, is not strictly classical in effect, but belongs to forms which are very irregular, never rectangular. In addition, breaks in the rectilinearity appear throughout; e.g. drapery forms bite into the columns, and smoke blurs the vertical lines of the colonnade above the staircase.[61] Between Guérin and Delacroix there have emerged romanticism and Orientalism, as well as that vogue for Gothic complication in which Delacroix also participated.[62]

Thus, it was from changed preconceptions rather than from a more critical knowledge that critics such as Baudelaire called Delacroix's temple "really patriarchal." The same change inspired Delacroix to find in the theatrical qualities of Oriental architecture a matter worth infusing with the spirit of Rubens. This combination produced the special quality of the architectural setting for the *Heliodorus*.

Although Delacroix's interest in French classic theater may have stimulated in him an interest in the Temple of Jerusalem, it cannot account for his turning to the Orient for convincingly "biblical" details. Here the artist felt the influence of the romantic theater, which had transformed the old classical décors through its quest for local color with convincing archaeological details and its demand that the characters be set in the actual milieu where they had lived.[63]

60. Hittorff, in *Restitution du Temple*, referred to the "observation made a long time ago" that "the Athenian cities and room interiors are very similar to those of the Moorish houses of Cairo and Algeria."

61. Cf., for this device, numerous 18th century religious paintings, as of Doyen, De Troy, et al.

62. As in his painting, *The Death of Valentine* (Salon of 1848), where, parenthetically, the flat molding on the window below and to the right closely resembles the upper left and right doorways in the *Heliodorus*. Also, compare the windows in the *Faust Attempting to Seduce Margaret*, a lithograph (1827, Delteil No. 65).

63. This is not to deny the presence of a minor but persistent strain of interest among classicists in Oriental motifs, which however were rarely the dominant aspect of major works. On the romantic theater see M. J. Moynet, *L'envers du théâtre*, Paris, 1875, 32. Also, cf. V. Hugo's *Préface de*

Delacroix had been brought into closer contact with the romantic theater through his collaboration with the romantic theatrical designer Cicéri (and with Cicéri's pupil Boulangé), and his use of architecture and its ornament to provide local color coincides with the intentions of romantic dramatists. However, the realism which documented his imagination had to be suggestive rather than literal, extraordinary or grotesque rather than commonplace or ugly, and he decried in his *Journal* on April 9, 1856 the excessive realism employed in staging Halévy's *La Juive*, in terms reminiscent of those he used with regard to realist painters.

Delacroix's Orientalism passed through two phases, before and after his trip to Morocco in 1832. The earlier phase culminated in the *Sardanapalus* (1827), whose "Assyrian" motifs he derived both from travel-book illustrations of Persepolis and from actual Persian miniatures.[64] From his Morocco trip Delacroix brought back fresh observations for his Oriental subjects. Henceforth until the end he drew on these sources, adding to them from time to time through the further study of travel books and their illustrations.

The decorative motifs for the *Heliodorus* (wholly different from those of the *Sardanapalus*) and the very concept of the great entering portal were strongly influenced, I believe, first by Delacroix's study of a portfolio of drawings from Persian architectural motifs and secondly by drawings and memories of the Moorish style of Africa and Spain, seen during the 1832 trip.[65]

Less than two weeks after noting in his *Journal* that he was working on the sketches for Saint-Sulpice, on March 11, 1850 Delacroix wrote at length about Persian architecture and its decoration: "...Next we saw a portfolio of drawings by a M. Laurens, who traveled in all these countries.[66] One thing above all which strikes me is the character of Persian architecture. Although in the Arab style, nevertheless everything has the special character of the country. The form of the cupolas and of the ogives, the details of the capitals, the ornaments, everything is original." After criticizing the comparatively dry architectural style of the West, which constantly returns to the "imitation of the antique," he continued: "I saw, among the drawings made in Persia, a complete entablature, with capitals, frieze, cornice, etc., entirely in the Greek proportions, but with ornaments which completely renew it and which are inventive." He concluded with a striking sentence, which seems directly related to the *Heliodorus:* "Keep in mind in the Persian drawings those immense portals *(immenses portails)* set before buildings which

Cromwell, ed. of Souriau, Paris, 1897, 265: "The drama must be radically impregnated with the color of its time."

64. See B. Farwell, "Sources for Delacroix's Death of Sardanapalus," *AB*, 40, 1958, 66-71. Also, see Lee Johnson, "Two Sources of Oriental Motifs Copied by Delacroix," *GBA*, 4th ser., 6, 1965, 163-68.

65. While Delacroix was probably aware of Botta's successive publications of *Nineveh* in 1843 and *Khorsabad* in 1847, he does not appear to have derived any motifs from the illustrations of these books.

66. Joubin's note on Laurens, in the *Journal*, I, 348, n. 2, reads: "Jules Laurens, 1825-1901, of Carpentras, accompanied the mission of Hommaire de Hell to Anatolia and Persia, as official painter, and had brought back from it numerous studies and drawings."

are actually smaller; it looks like huge operatic scenery set up in front of the building. I know of no other example of this anywhere."

A number of Laurens's illustrations were published in 1853 in Hommaire de Hell's *Voyage en Turquie et Perse* (Figs. 72-75). Among the illustrations some are significantly similar to the architecture and decoration of the *Heliodorus*.[67]

Moorish architecture, with which the artist was acquainted,[68] may have served as a link between Laurens's Persian drawings and Delacroix's Temple of Jerusalem. Both the complicated contours of a Moorish archway and the patterned decoration of the walls in a wash drawing (Louvre, RF 9265) made in Morocco or Spain prefigure in a general way corresponding details of the Temple. On the wall in the right corner of the *A Street in Meknes* (1832) and in the left corner of the *Women of Algiers* (1834) appears an octagonal motif almost identical with that of a drawing for the mural (Fig. 52) which was not used; and in a volume probably known to Delacroix and published in Paris in 1849[69] there is a drawing of a frieze on a Moorish building which closely resembles a floral motif on the balcony frieze of the *Heliodorus*. It is now clearer what relevance Persian architecture had for Delacroix's Jewish Temple: in his mind there was a connection between Moorish and Persian architecture on the one hand—he actually called Persian architecture "Arab in style"—and between the styles of the Moors and the Jews on the other; hence, he turned for inspiration to Laurens's Persian drawings as a way to give his temple more biblical authenticity.

67. Pl. IX (Fig. 72), "Crypte Byzantine. Taillée dans la Montagne à Midiah [Roumélie]." Note that while not all of the illustrations are from Persia proper (this one is from Bulgaria), they nevertheless share common stylistic qualities. The contours of the capitals in this illustration have a character very like that of Delacroix's temple. In pl. XLII (Fig. 73), "Cour de la Grande Mosquée à Diarbékir," the variations of the shafts of the columns and some of the irregularly shaped corbelings or arches resemble those in sketches for Delacroix's temple. Pl. XXIV (Fig. 74), "Debris Romains et du Moyen Age à Amasserah," may have provided a link in Delacroix's mind between Laurens's illustrations and his *Heliodorus*, since there appears the classic theme of a mounted soldier over a fallen enemy, not unlike the angel rider over Heliodorus. In pl. XXV (Fig. 75), "Cheminée Turque à Tcherchembèh," the elaborately curved contours of the chimney suggest the unusual contours of the spandrels in the lower doors of the *Heliodorus*, particularly the round swelling forms at the bases of the spandrels. The standing man's beard and moustache

resemble Onias'. In addition, the writhing bands which decorate the panels beside the edge of the chimney resemble the snake form of the *Heliodorus* spandrel, especially in some early sketches. Delacroix first discovered this kind of complicated profile in Algeria, and he used it several times in his earlier work to suggest an Oriental flavor; e.g. the watercolor, *The House of the Jewish Wedding*, 1832 (Louvre, RF 3375); the drawing of a Dominican convent in Madrid, 1832 (Louvre, RF 9254), No. 177 in Sérullaz, *Mémorial Delacroix*; *The Moroccan Family*, 1833, No. 222 in the *Delacroix Ausstellung*, Bremen, 1964 (private coll., Bremen); and *The Jewish Wedding*, 1841 Salon (Louvre).

68. Delacroix's knowledge and admiration of this style is evident in his *Journal* entry made in Seville on May 26, 1832: "Alcazar: superb Moorish style different from the monuments of Africa."

69. Charles Texier, *Description de l'Asie Mineure faite par ordre du Gouvernement Français de 1833 à 1837*, Paris, 1849, III, "Aspendus. Pl. 240 Détail de l'entablature Ionique." Delacroix referred to Texier in his article "Des variations du

Despite Delacroix's great attraction to Oriental decorative motifs for details his Temple of Jerusalem remains basically Western: he viewed Jewish architecture with French eyes much as he had done on his trip to Africa in 1832, when he filled his notebooks with references to France and to European art. His criticism of the Western architectural style was selective and directed chiefly against bad imitations of the antique (which included the sixteenth century).[70] Delacroix's interest in Persian architecture seems to be centered on the later style, with its many Roman elements; and his appreciation of it in Laurens's illustrations was doubly selective, since he saw the architecture through the eyes of a French compatriot.[71] There is evidence for another connection with contemporary French taste—very difficult to establish, however—in Delacroix's comparison of the Persian architecture in Laurens's drawings to "operatic scenery." The opera, no less than the theater, probably inspired the artist's imagination, since he was fond of attending both and often studied their stage settings.[72] One is not surprised to find that many of Delacroix's contemporaries, even knowledgeable travelers such as Edouard Charton (1807-1890), who, basing himself on illustrations of columns published in his journal which purported to be from the Temple of Jerusalem and which resembled those in the *Heliodorus*, literally believed that Delacroix had through imagination represented the original Temple architecture in his *Heliodorus*.[73] It may be more than a coincidence that the man whose words and pictures described these ancient remains in Charton's journal was Alexandre Bida (1823-1895), one of Delacroix's pupils (see Figs. 76 and 77). The assumption that the capitals from Delacroix's

beau," *Revue des deux mondes*, in the context of a discussion of Jewish architecture.

70. In his will, written in August 1863, the artist required that his tomb be "copied very exactly after the antique, either Vignola or Palladio, with very pronounced projections, contrary to everything that is done today in architecture." See for the original text Philippe Burty, *Lettres de Eugène Delacroix (1815-1863)*, Paris, Quantin, 1878, vii. Indeed, the usually perceptive Escholier overlooked all of Delacroix's Orientalism and referred to the architecture of the *Heliodorus* as "Palladian," in his book *Delacroix*, III, 107.

71. Delacroix, in the entry of March 11, 1850, before enthusiastically discussing Laurens's sketches, dismissed some original Persian drawings as having "neither perspective nor any feeling for real painting, that is, a certain illusion of projection, etc.: the figures are unmoving, the poses awkward...." However, Delacroix did appreciate other Persian paintings, from which he actually borrowed motifs.

72. Professor André Racz of Columbia, sensing Masonic tendencies in Delacroix like those in

Mozart, first suggested the *Magic Flute* as an inspiration for Delacroix since the artist was fond of the overture and since there are certain similarities between the wording of his text explaining the Apollo ceiling (which I have linked to the *St. Michael*) and phrases in the opera. The Temple of Wisdom of the opera was equated by the revolutionaries of 1789 with Solomon's Temple; in fact, a standard early translation into French was made in 1801. For my part, I have tried (aided by the *conservateur* of the Bibliothèque de l'Opéra and of the librarian of the Mozarteum in Salzburg) unsuccessfully to find illustrations of Parisian opera stage settings.

73. See below, Appendix III, for Charton's statement, cited by Thoré in his article on Delacroix's chapel decorations. Edouard Charton edited *Le tour du monde*, which appeared twice a year. The pieces of columns referred to are in the first semester of 1860, "Voyages en Palestine, 1856-59. inédits. 15 jours à Jérusalem." Bida, the illustrator, remarked on p. 391: "I visited (in 1856) the Mosque of 'El Aqsa; underground vaults located below the Temple of Solomon. I draw there two col-

72 Hommaire de Hell, *Voyage en Turquie et Perse*, 1853, Pl. IX, "Crypte Byzantine. Taillée dans la Montagne à Midiah [Roumélie]"

73 Hommaire de Hell, *Voyage en Turquie et Perse*, 1853, Pl. XLII, "Cour de la Grande Mosquée à Diarbékir"

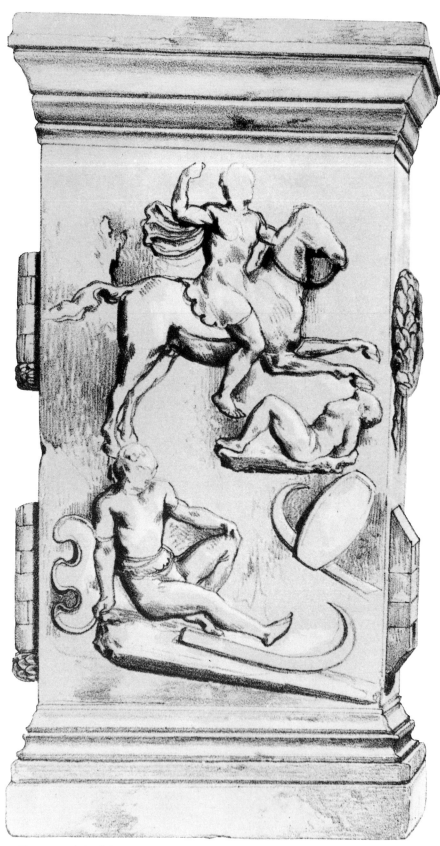

74 Hommaire de Hell, *Voyage en Turquie et Perse*, 1853, Pl. XXIV, "Debris Romains
et du Moyen Age à Amasserah"

75 Hommaire de Hell, *Voyage en Turquie et Perse*, 1853, Pl. XXV, "Cheminée Turque à Tcherchembèh"

TRICHON

76 Bida, "Voyages en Palestine, 1856-9...," *Le tour du monde*, 1st sem., 1860, p. 495: "Un pilier dans le souterrain du temple de Jérusalem"

TRICHON

77 Bida, "Voyages en Palestine, 1856-9...," *Le tour du monde*, 1st. sem., 1860, p. 496: "Autre pilier dans le souterrain du temple de Salomon"

Temple and those from the underground vault of 'El Aqsa noted by Charton were both authentically biblical shows, in fact, that in this instance the imagination of the artist and the opinion of the archaeologist were grounded in the same preconceptions.

In the *Jacob*, Delacroix went one step beyond the moralized landscapes of the romantic writers and painters by adding what his contemporaries considered Oriental magnificence. Some critics greeted the landscape as "truly biblical" and others, calling it "poetically biblical," still recognized its touch of authenticity.[74] However, their opinions, as in the case of the *Heliodorus*, were grounded not on more accurate knowledge of the biblical epoch, but on the belief that biblical dress and physiognomy survived among the contemporary Jews living in the "unchanging" lands of the newly revealed Near East.[75] This intense interest in Near Eastern lands and peoples stimulated the combination of sentimentality and realism in the Orientalist paintings of artists like Marilhat and the well-known Horace Vernet (1789-1863), who remarked of Algeria in 1830: "It was Jacob and the whole of Genesis…what a beautiful painting."[76] Actually Vernet's Oriental landscapes were drily documentary rather than beautiful, and set a style characterized by monotonously sun-blanched, arid deserts. Delacroix, on the other hand, based his local color on the imaginative use of documentation such as the drawings of travelers and the engravings illustrating their books; and for his landscape in the *Jacob* he most probably also drew on his own strong impressions received on the trip to Morocco in 1832.[77] But we have seen earlier that special qualities of the landscape in the *Jacob*, as in some other works of the mid-1850's with imaginative or exotic settings, owe most to his intimate and perceptive observation of oak trees in the forest of Sénart at Champrosay.[78] This last point went unnoticed by his contemporaries, for many of whom Delacroix's French forest, spiced with Oriental flowers

umns, one of them certainly going back to the magnificent king. It is perhaps the only ornamentation remaining of the Hebrew epoch. These constructions are gigantic." The illustrations on pp. 405f., both by Bida, are of columns in the "underground vaults of the Temple of Jerusalem."

74. See below, Chapter IV, and Appendix III for the critical views.

75. North Africa was virgin territory to most Frenchmen before Napoleon's Egyptian campaign, as we have seen, revealed it to the campaigners directly, and to the rest of France indirectly through engravings. Algeria was opened up and became accessible to travelers only in the 1830's.

76. For the full text of Vernet's remark, and references, see Jean Alazard, *L'Orient et la peinture française au XIXe siècle*, Paris, 1930, 131.

77. For the Morocco trip's influence on the landscape of the *Jacob*, see Prosper Dorbec, "Le paysage dans l'oeuvre d'Eugène Delacroix," *GBA*, 5th ser., 11, 1925, 141. In a notebook preserved at the Cabinet des Dessins, Louvre, "Voyage au Maroc," 1712 bis, on the page inscribed "11 Avril à Eüs Daliah," appears a scene in watercolor with elements quite similar to the landscape of the *Jacob*: below and to the right of a high, green clump of trees, centrally placed and with vistas on both sides, passes a line of horsemen. The arrangement of two trees on a hill leaning against the frame to the right with sky visible on either side seems to have attracted the artist, for a sketch illustrated under No. 626 of Robaut essentially repeats it. That Delacroix continued to think of his 1832 trip during the early stages of composing the *Jacob* is shown by the list of studies made in Morocco, which Delacroix entered in the *Journal* in 1850-52. See *Journal*, III, 437-38. It should also be noted that Delacroix painted in 1849 a variant (Robaut 1077) of his

and other details drawn from his own observations and readings, seemed profoundly authentic.

The combination in the *Jacob* of influences from the old masters with directly perceived details places the artist in a tradition going at least as far back as Titian but kept alive in the nineteenth century by writers familiar to Delacroix such as Burnet (basing himself on Reynolds), and by such artists as Constable, for whom the goal of art was "to unite imagination with nature."[79] This was the attitude of Horace Vernet, who said, "When I want to paint, I stick my head out the window," as well as of Delacroix, who often sketched outside of the studio and recorded many perceptions of nature, but who was mainly guided by imagination when composing.[80] For the romantic landscapists in general, details of local color were often inserted into a previously determined composition, which was itself sometimes a variant of an older master's arrangement. Théodore Rousseau, for instance, continually referred to older Flemish or French masters, and despite his efforts to capture the accidental, changeful look of nature, often placed monumental form and harmonious composition first, even before color; still, this independent artist, by the example of his direct and vigorous landscapes, may have encouraged Delacroix to his most advanced effort in the genre, that of the *Jacob*.[81] The artists had admired one another's work for several years at least, when an exhibition of the landscapist's work held in Paris in February 1850, the first in two decades, impressed Delacroix with its originality just as he was working on his sketches for Saint-Sulpice.[82] Sketching for himself in the forest near Champrosay, Delacroix came at times close to the spirit of the painters of Barbizon (he knew and admired the work of Diaz as well as of Rousseau), and it was to this facet of his art, rather than to his taste for curving lines ("the arabesque of the line") repeated rhythmically in several parts of the composition, that he owed the robust quality of the landscape in the *Jacob*; its trees

Women of Algiers (1834, Louvre).

78. Théophile Silvestre, the artist's friend, stated that Delacroix based the forest scene of *Weislingen Captured by Götz's Men* on the forest of Sénart. See Silvestre's *Eugène Delacroix. Documents nouveaux*, Paris, 1864, 51-58, cited by Lee Johnson in his scholarly catalogue for the Delacroix show at the Art Gallery of Toronto, December 1, 1962. The *Lion and Cayman*, 1855 (Louvre), also has a number of resemblances to the *Jacob* and to the landscapes in the Cabinet des Dessins notebook and in Robaut No. 626.

79. See John Burnet, "Practical Hints on Light and Shade," in *Practical Essays on Art*, London, 1893, 31: "Reynolds mentions a mode of composing by taking a figure from some celebrated master, and designing others to correspond with it; thereby imparting a grandeur of style to the whole. So, by commencing with something sketched from nature, we give a decided look of truth to the

other parts of the picture." On Constable, see Leslie, *Memoirs of ... John Constable*, 195, citing a letter of September 1829.

80. On Horace Vernet, see Charles Blanc, *Une famille d'artistes: les 3 Vernet: Joseph—Carle—Horace*, Paris, 1928, 128. Among other references to open air by Delacroix, see the *Journal*, September 7, 1856.

81. On Rousseau's theories and practice, see Philippe Burty, *Maîtres et petits-maîtres*, Paris, 1877, 120-60.

82. See the *Journal* for February 24 and 27 and March 1, 1850. For Rousseau's appreciation of Delacroix, who, "with all his faults and exaggerations," is "powerful as a voice from Dante's Inferno," see Burty, *Maîtres*, 157-59. For a discussion of the contacts between the two artists, which date back to the early 1840's, see Pierre Angrand, "Théodore Rousseau et Eugène Delacroix," *GBA*, 6th ser., 68, 1966, 215-61.

especially have an immediacy that mark a decisive break with older models such as those of Titian and Rubens.[83] The artist showed himself in profound sympathy with these sturdy contemporaries (including Corot, whose trees he admired in 1847) in the tangible reality of his oaks, which are so near to the foreground that their wrinkled texture and irregular edges are clearly visible, and which belong neither to the biblical, Renaissance nor Baroque epochs, but to the nineteenth century.[84] Thus Delacroix, while consciously aiming—like the older masters he revered—to produce a grand and imposing effect, chose a means which Rousseau himself could respect, in giving the spectator a close-up of the majestic trees which, he felt, would have looked much less impressive from a distance.[85] One can find decided resemblances between the *Jacob* and certain landscapes of Rousseau in the posture and form of the trees, and in the coloring of the sky (the first among his decorations to be reddish), but Delacroix's landscape is nonetheless a distinctive achievement.[86] While Delacroix appreciated aspects of the lighting and color of Rousseau's landscapes (he is even said to have called his own "dull" in comparison) and pursued a similar goal of romantic awesomeness through massive forms and dramatic lighting, his own late landscapes introduced new qualities of form and lighting. Particularly in his landscape of the *Jacob*—perhaps because he was stimulated by its challenge as mural decoration—Delacroix departed in his work significantly from Rousseau's in giving it a considerably lighter, less somber look and in interpreting the sculptural masses of the trees in terms of colored reflections and shadows.[87] Thus, despite the biblical exoticism of his subjects and his debts to older masters in form, Delacroix, through his vivid details painted with rich brushwork, his strong color contrasts and his bright palette, pointed beyond the chiaroscuro of the Barbizon master toward Impressionism.[88]

B. COMPOSITION AND COLOR

"If to a composition already interesting by the choice of subject, you add an arrangement of lines which augments the impression, a chiaroscuro striking to the imagination, a color adapted to the characters, you have resolved a more difficult problem, and once more you are superior: it is a harmony and variations adapted to a unique melody..." (Eugène Delacroix).[89]

83. Dorbec, "Le paysage dans l'oeuvre d'Eugène Delacroix," *GBA*, 5th ser., 11, 1925, 125-44, refers to Delacroix's study of the tree lighting in Rousseau, Diaz and Corot. See *Journal*, October 8, 1847. Professor Julius S. Held rightly sensed that there might be some connection between the trees in the *Jacob* and the Barbizon painters, and suggested it to me.

84. On Corot, see *Journal*, March 14, 1847.

85. On the grandeur of trees when seen close up, see the *Journal*, May 9, 1853. For a discussion, with brief bibliography, of scale and "the sub-

lime" in relation to the trees of *Jacob*, see Mras, *Delacroix's Theory of Art*, 22-23.

86. For a similar red sky behind greenish foliage, see e.g. Rousseau's *Sunset, Fontainebleau*, bought by the State in 1848 and exhibited in the Salon of 1851 and possibly also among the paintings seen by Delacroix in February 1850. The overlapping of the trees and their imposing height, with their crowns filling the upper third of the painting, are comparable to the *Jacob*.

87. See the *Journal*, May 5, 1852 and April 29, 1854.

88. On Rousseau's own anticipation of the new

The first impression of intense drama presented by each of Delacroix's three chapel paintings leads the spectator to sense their unity. The straight lines of the architecture in the *Heliodorus* form a golden-gray stage where a crowd of protagonists acts; the curving green vegetation of the *Jacob* surrounds a pair of isolated wrestlers; the smoldering rocky ground and burning sky of the *St. Michael* are a tempestuous arena wherein two great angels fight. Furthermore, there are parallels in the forms of the paintings: the two major figures, of the same size in all the paintings, are set close to the foreground; their engagement takes place on a flat area raised like a dais above the lower edge of the frame and tilted at about the same angle in each case; and the smoky sky of the *St. Michael* contains small articulated forms very much like those in the other two paintings. Obviously there are major differences in subject and in coloring among the murals; and in addition the heavy frame of the *St. Michael*, which has already been discussed, sets the painting off from the others through its oval shape and gold coloring. However, the close examination and comparison of the paintings which will be made in this chapter will reveal other, less obvious aspects of the chapel's unity.

1. Composition

a) Gesture and Line

The most powerful movement in the *Heliodorus*, the thrust of the upper drapery to the right, which is channeled down toward Heliodorus along the column, the balcony and the whipping angel, plays an important role within the composition; indeed, with such gestures Delacroix unified the scene dramatically: a punitive spirit seems to sweep down past the curtain, which whirls in its wake, and to penetrate the open arms of its victim. The artist's use of drapery for these interconnected gestures and for curving movements which flow across the forms tying them together brings him closer to the Baroque and Rococo than to the sculpturesque tradition of the Italian Renaissance with its massive forms composed discretely.[90] The proportions of the large movements and masses to the small active parts sometimes—as in the corkscrew sash on the left angel's back and the straying forelocks of the right angel—lack the dignity of the Italian masters, whose grave, decorously designed shapes suited the statuesque bodies they covered.

style—different from Delacroix's—see Thomas Paulsson, "From Rousseau to Pissarro," *Figura*, New Series, 1, 1959, 204-18. For an earlier appreciation of Rousseau's "revolutionary" role, see Rosenthal, *Du romantisme*, 293.

89. See the *Journal*, May 20, 1853.

90. One thinks at once of Rubens' draperies, and even—despite Delacroix's aversion to their art—of Boucher's or Fragonard's. Neoclassic drapery, placed before bare backgrounds, often seemed to gesticulate meaninglessly, as in David's *Tennis Court Oath* (1790), in which the large billowing curtain at the upper left is isolated from the turbulent crowd below by the stern blank wall. With Gros, and especially with Géricault, drapery served not only dramatically as in David, but compositionally as in the 17th century. For his ability to unite figure and background, Rembrandt was especially admired by Delacroix, as noted in Mras, *Delacroix's Theory of Art*, 110. Otto Benesch asserted that in some small late paintings of religious subjects Delacroix shows his increasing spiritualization by actually turning "from his idol Rubens to Rembrandt" ("Rem-

In attempting to unify his big "machine," Delacroix relied considerably on accessories, interpreted not only as texture but as gesture. Believing that "a very small [badly made] accessory will sometimes destroy the effect of a whole painting," he exerted much care not only in the drapery but in the decorations of the architecture and the clothing and in the arrangement of such objects as the pieces of treasure lying in two heaps on the bottom steps and spotted along the whole lower half of the painting.[91] These details were intended to perform the important functions of setting the stage for the main actors in the drama, of emphasizing and clarifying their gestures and of unifying the composition. In this respect, such secondary gestures as those of Onias and the woman beside him, and of the woman and child at the top of the steps, which participate in or echo the curtain's thrust, function as "accessories" to the "figure" of the big drapery.[92] Even the decoration, which tattoos armor and treasure, cloak and wall alike, plays a role in the drama and helps to unify the composition through analogies among the motifs: the band that runs along the walls and is prominent on the central column reappears on the large vase in the lower left corner and suggests a snipping from the larger form on the central receding wall. The latter form resembles the snake on the panel behind the upper angel's left leg, and the form of the snake itself, which is poking its head into a floral shape, is echoed by the plant forms above.

Besides the decoration, which in Delacroix's hands becomes dynamic, other apparently static forms enter the drama either by being aligned with or helping to emphasize the gestures of the figures: the platter in the lower left corner juts to the right along the stair tread (parallel to a series of round forms culminating in the angel's face above) and thereby ties the whole group to the main action; the blue band above the horse's head reinforces the powerful arching of its neck; and the complicated outline of the wall panel behind the upper angel's left leg underlines his body's movement.

Realistic detail in the landscape of the *Jacob*, as in the temple of the *Heliodorus*, has no less a dramatic or compositional than an archaeological intention. The giant French trees impress us by their power; and the still life, which contains a hat and cloak probably closer in fashion to Rococo models than to ancient biblical ones, by being placed in the lower right-hand corner helps to activate this large empty area and serves as an attractive entry into the painting.

In unifying the composition of the *Jacob*, Delacroix faced different problems from those of the *Heliodorus*. With its round, organic forms, the landscape seems comparatively incoherent

brandt's Artistic Heritage. II. From Goya to Cézanne," *GBA*, 6th ser., 56, 1960, 101-16, esp. 110).

91. See the *Journal*, September 23, 1846 for the remark on accessories.

92. Delacroix regarded accessories not as absolute, but as relative to other forms. Thus, he said that "not only...the small details, the backgrounds, but the figures themselves may be accessories." See the *Journal*, July 3, 1858.

beside the flat walls and ground of the temple. The trunks do not extend the whole height of the painting, as the columns almost do, nor are there spectators viewing the main action and giving a dramatic unity to the scene; hence the need for such devices as the spear, added at a late stage in order to link the still life to the wrestlers and to guide the eye from the lower frame into the painting. The motion of the caravan provides another impulse in a counterclockwise direction for the viewer's eye, which enters the composition along the right edge and thus, like the spear, helps link the lower and middle regions of the painting. Certain larger forms, by repeating the curve of the top of the frame, connect the middle to the upper regions of the composition: the curving ground under and over the wrestlers and the arc of the tree branches over their heads. But the painting contains few massive stabilizing objects; neither the trees, wrestlers, caravan, hills, nor mountains are parallel to the sides of the frame. To balance these dynamically inclined forms and hold the composition together, the artist introduced analogies among the smaller forms in movement, line, color and brush work. One is struck by the advanced character of the composition implied by the artist's relying on "microstructure" (as the Impressionists will do) to bind the forms together; but it must be remembered that this method grew mainly out of the exigencies of the large surface to be decorated, not primarily from a wish to show forms dissolved in light, and that these small forms are unifying details sprinkled over massive shapes otherwise having insufficient coherence. Furthermore, as will appear presently from an analysis of details in the *Heliodorus* and in the *Jacob*, while Delacroix often built up his forms out of varied overlays of pigment and complex webs of hatching, his brush strokes mainly suggest handwriting or scribblings (as in some Manet lithographs) and only secondarily the Impressionist analysis of light into small irregular dots and commas.

Just as in the *Heliodorus*, many repetitions of movement and gesture among the accessories help to unify the *Jacob*: the convergent interlocking of the wrestlers' bodies inverts the divergent spreading apart of the trees (unlike some sketches—discussed in Chapter II—in which the trees also interlock); Jacob's leftward lunge has a modified echo in the shepherd's position and movement; and the similarly bent tree limbs, which gesticulate like the balcony figures in the *Heliodorus*, draw the eye into a counterclockwise rotation that grazes the frame. The dramatic triangle, whose vertex is the clasped hands of the wrestlers, finds many echoes throughout the painting: in the sky over the wrestlers, between the trees, and in their branches, and in the large sunlit region of the caravan, bordered by foliage and the curving hillside.

An arabesque line serves at once to vary and unite the surface. The contrast of straight and curved is beautifully exploited in the still life, in which the scarf curls around the shaft of the spear, and in the first and third tree trunks, whose long lines are interrupted by curving masses of vines. A series of parallel serpentine forms is repeated in different regions: Jacob's robe, the path from the tree to the hill, from the woman to the road and from the hat to the scarf. The frayed end of the scarf in the still life resembles the lion's foot on the border of Jacob's cloak. An implied rhythmical line results from the placement of a series of white and off-white accents along the angel's robe and Jacob's leggings. In many places, apparent complexity is achieved by a masterful use of line, as in the flat areas of foliage, whose luxuriance depends not so much on internal variations in the masses of leaves as on the suggestive variety and energy of the outermost leaf edges.

b) Scale and Viewpoint

The life-size scale of the main figures in the three paintings makes them seem credible beings, within the same space as the spectator. That Delacroix worried about harmonizing his paintings through the scale of the figures is clear from the several versions of the *St. Michael*, in which he altered significantly the proportions of the main figures. The smaller scale of the secondary figures (the caravan which dwindles to a series of dots in the distance; Onias and the figures about him; the remote demons on the ground) seems to be intended to restore an impressiveness to the scale of the background forms (the trees, the temple, the earth), which suffers from the large size of the main figures. (Delacroix's concern about the effect of the scale of the individual figure within the painting as well as of the painting as a whole within its setting becomes clear on reading his discussion in the *Journal* of October 20, 1853.) We may wonder whether in the ratio of the size of the figures to the size of the painting there is a scale characteristic of the mid-nineteenth century as distinguished from one characteristic of the Renaissance or of the Baroque epoch. I cannot here answer this interesting question, which would require further definitions of the periods as well as the comparison of accurate measurements of many paintings.

Delacroix placed the horizon lines of the *Jacob* and of the *Heliodorus* on the same level, giving the small region of flat ground-plane on which the wrestlers stand a position and slope similar to that of the dais of the temple; consequently, the spectator finds the perspective system of the *Heliodorus* roughly approximated in the *Jacob*, although it lacks straight converging lines. As will appear presently, the artist aimed to be decoratively pleasing by taking into account both the harmony of the colors and the visibility of the paintings (in terms of their light and brush strokes); indeed, having experienced similar problems in his earlier projects, Delacroix was quite conscious of the chapel as an architectural space to be decorated, in distinction to easel paintings, and—a point discussed earlier—realizing that his drawings and even his first sketches on the wall could only approximate the final appearance of the murals when in place, he anticipated retouching the paintings when he could examine them with the scaffolding removed.

The average eye-level of a person standing in the chapel is six to seven feet below the horizon line of the paintings. If Delacroix had completely adjusted his murals to the spectator, he would have adopted those spectacular optical devices of the Renaissance and later periods that cause paintings to "fall through" the architecture and (as in Raphael's fresco) make the depicted space seem an extension of real space. Such an approach would probably have conflicted with that powerful urge to self-assertion which induced the artist to letter his name in large monumental characters on the *Heliodorus* and to produce these self-contained paintings, detached from the architecture by wide frames, in which the figures—unlike some figures in Raphael's version, which stare out at the spectator—seem aware only of the drama in which they are acting.

Viewers can sense a conflict between the scale of the paintings, which brings them into relation with a spectator in the chapel, and the high viewpoint and the self-containment of the drama, which isolate them from him. One might say that Delacroix's sense of decorative fitness and his grasp of reality induced him to consider the spectator, whereas his imagination led him away, toward his private fantasy.

c) Light and Shadow

The main source of light of both the *Heliodorus* and the *Jacob* comes from the direction of the window which illuminates the chapel (an arrangement as old as the Renaissance), thereby, like the scale, aligning the paintings with some aspect of the room; however, it has already been mentioned that both paintings exhibit inconsistencies in their lighting. In the *Heliodorus* the primary light defines the architectural masses and spaces, but a secondary different source of light emphasizes the main group in the foreground, as with a spotlight. Indeed, since the artist's purpose is not only to reproduce realistic lighting, there occur discrepancies between the shadows implied by the light sources and those actually cast: the whip of the left angel, held in his left hand, casts no shadow, although it is directly over the angel's back (the angel's sash does cast a shadow on his cloak); Heliodorus' right leg casts a strong shadow on the steps, whereas the whipping angel at about twice the distance above Heliodorus, and in the light, casts no shadow on him. The shadows are often rounded, softened forms with reduced shapes which do not exactly reproduce the shapes of the subjects casting them. Lighter shadows characterize the late style of the artist, and Delacroix actually referred in his *Journal* on March 24, 1855, to a change from the handling of his earlier paintings which he criticized for having "black shadows."[93]

However much Delacroix lightened his cast shadows (in this respect anticipating Impressionism), he adhered basically to a tradition of sculptural modeling, of chiaroscuro. For him shading, which belongs to solid bodies as the local color yellow belongs to gold, might be described as the "local color" of solidity. The case is identical with his foreshortenings and recessions, which function as the "local color" of perspective.[94] When introducing lights and shadows, the artist considered their direction, size and shape not only in relation to correct lighting but as compositional inventions, or as dramatic emphases; thus, he reduced the shadows around the faces of the three angels, giving them an unworldly glow. However, Delacroix on the whole remained within the bounds of credibility; thus, wishing to emphasize the dramatic movement of the drapery, he introduced a strong contrast between the brightly lighted side facing the sun and the deep pocket of shadow on the other side, and, wanting to brighten certain areas of the architecture, he placed in front of them the glittering head on the soldier's spear (a late idea, evolved in the sketches), and the shining limbs of the downward-hurtling angel.

The whole grouping of lights and darks, combined with such strong dramatic movements as those of the figures on the steps and of the drapery, solves in the tradition of Rubens and the Venetians a problem in composition which plagued many of Delacroix's contemporaries: how to unite the lighted main action below to the bright areas above (sky, angels). The superiority of his solution, which avoids the dark pockets of shadow of other artists, can be gauged from photographs of the paintings exhibited at the Universal Exhibition of 1855 in Paris.[95]

The same liberties with the logic of light and shadow—which have more to do with producing a successful decoration than with reproducing a Near Eastern dawn—heighten the dramatic effects of the *Jacob*.[96] Indeed, the critics (cited in Appendix III) gave three different accounts of

93. Cf. *Journal*, January 11, 1857: "Shadows. There are no shadows, properly speaking, only reflections. Importance of setting definite limits to the shadows. They are always too strong."

94. In contradiction to the view that Delacroix was indifferent to the question of perspective, since he "makes mistakes" in the *Heliodorus*, there are diagrams of one- and two-point perspective on a sketch for this painting in the Louvre, RF 10, 147 (Figs. 64, 65). See the discussion in Chapter II.

95. For illustrations reproduced from originals at the Eastman House, see the article by Frank Trapp,

its lighting: Baudelaire, who may have derived his idea from the biblical text, exulted over its "lights of morning"; Merson criticized the contradiction that "the sun sets in the background and rises in the foreground"; and Vitet complained that "it is earliest dawn that the combat should finish and his painting is illuminated rather like high noon." This use of multiple lighting sources to heighten the drama belongs especially within the Venetian colorist tradition, and was just the aspect of Titian's *St. Peter Martyr* which Fuseli praised as "assisting and invigorating the effect, without impairing the unity."[97]

Certain sketches for the *Jacob*, such as the oil in Vienna, with their strong contrasts of color and lighting are more dramatic than the mural itself, whose large surfaces required that Delacroix narrow the range of light values and avoid discontinuities. His goal of brightness without monotony could only be achieved through his mastery of color.

2. Color

a) The Relation of Color to Composition

The color of the *Heliodorus,* one of the most exciting and enjoyable features of the painting, also contributes to the effectiveness of the composition. The initial impression received by persons used to modern painting is of an overall grayness; but examination quickly reveals that the gray includes color contrasts masterfully harmonized, and that strong touches of color in objects spotted over the painting evoke an appropriately luxuriant atmosphere. An essential function of these color placements is to enhance the decoration; e.g. Delacroix "invented" the brown-skinned man on the balcony whose small round face sets off the big vermilion region of the drapery.

Color functions in the drama (like the linear patterns and gestures already discussed) by uniting or detaching figures and objects as the action demands it; thus, by the use of like hues for different objects which are dramatically connected, Delacroix strengthened and clarified their relations. The gold vase which burdens the soldier at the right has its "moral antithesis" on the left in the gold miter which helps propel upward the girl who is running on the stairs behind the horseman. As she runs upstairs imploring help, her dark blue dress is similarly "answered" by the down-hurtling purple-blue form of the chastising angel symmetrically disposed in front of the horse. The division of her dress into two colors corresponds to the contrast of the red drapery above and the blue cloak of the angel below: her red-brown waist closely resembles the similarly colored garb of the man on the landing toward whom she mounts,

"The Universal Exhibition of 1855," *BurlM, 107,* 1965, 300-305. One notes that the same high form with round top of Delacroix's two facing paintings seems to have been adopted often for the religious paintings exhibited.

96. Bernard Denvir has rightly pointed out that Delacroix's paintings of African scenes are far less realistic than the notebook illustrations, and that the artist's light and shadow have less to do with Africa than with Veronese. See "Delacroix in Morocco," *The Geographical Magazine,* London, March 1949, 433-40.

97. See Fuseli's *Lectures,* 485-86.

whereas her dark blue skirt resembles the dark of the horse's tail and the green of the angel's dress below her. The whole group around Onias is united by a series of analogous colors in their dress (blue, green and purple); and the sanctum above Onias has a purple so close to the color of the High Priest's garb that one senses the intention to link the priest to the sanctum before which he gesticulates. The blue-purple cloak of the angel on the right continues the arc of the horse's dark blue mane and thereby connects his vertical movement with the horizontal gesture of the horse. The dull brown color of the whip in the right hand of the angel on the left points to and overlaps the still life below him, thus coupling the yellows of the golden objects with his light yellow-orange skin and suggesting a homily on Heliodorus' misbehavior: "My right hand points to this treasure which you have tried to steal, my left hand is about to whip you for it."[98]

The discussion so far has been concerned with the "macrostructure" of colors and their decorative and dramatic functions: but it is necessary to consider here the "microstructure" (a word applied earlier to the *Jacob*) of color spots sprinkled over these larger areas, a device which originated essentially in naturalism.[99] Thus, Delacroix seems to have introduced these varicolored dots in order to interpret his observation (in part originating in the theory of atmospheric perspective) that light is scattered into particles by the "atmosphere that envelops objects."[100] He determined the color of these spots by a rule also concerned with the observation of nature: "Every reflection has some green, every edge of a shadow, some violet."[101] Delacroix applied this rule in many places, e.g. in the rider's head and in his breastplate, which —although they are not next to objects with a green color—show green-tinged reflections; in the tilted platter in the corner whose purple gems are duller in the yellow light and intenser in the violet shadow; and in the rider's baton, which has purple-brown margins of shadow, a green half-light, a golden-yellow local color and a highlight of white with a trace of yellow tinting. Such a rule sounds restrictive, but the artist did not apply it systematically, and in fact he added a second rule which allowed him much greater leeway in his handling of reflections: "The more an object is polished or shiny, the less one sees the true color: it becomes a mirror which reflects the surrounding colors."[102] This rule enabled him to enhance the colors in many places, e.g. in the skirt of the girl running upstairs (its pattern of loops becomes yellow in the sunlight, orange where it faces the angel's red-tinted wings, while the blue skirt facing the wings is

98. The inclusion of objects which explain the "moral" of a picture was common up to the 19th century. John Burnet, "Practical Hints on Composition in Painting," *Practical Essays on Art*, London, 1893, 10, in discussing a Brouwer painting of peasants fighting, remarks that the cards thrown to the ground explain the cause of the fight.

99. Delacroix's openness to the realist tendencies of his day—already discussed—were evident to certain contemporaries, particularly in contrast to Ingres; thus, Louis Peisse in his *Salon de 1852* opposed the former's "realism" to the latter's "idealism." For an interpretation of the dots as *pointilliste* (no doubt derived from Signac's recently published book), see L.-E. Fournier, "Eugène Delacroix et ses peintures décoratives à St.-Sulpice," *Revue des arts décoratifs*, 21, 1901, 221-30.

100. See the *Journal*, January 25, 1857.

101. See *Journal*, January 13, 1857, and Andrieu, "Les

slightly purple); the face of the brown man beside the great drapery (its reddish spots presumably are reflected from the drapery); and a gray riser in the left corner (its yellow tinge is a reflection from the golden platter beside it). Reflections also supplement chiaroscuro and brushstroke techniques in adding to the solidity of some forms; e.g. Heliodorus' breastplate, which by reflecting the red cloth beneath it gains salience and is detached from the gray stairs.

From all this it is clear that the concern for reality implied by Delacroix's rules is balanced in practice by compositional and decorative interests; indeed, for his ceiling at the Hôtel de Ville he explicitly departed from the "natural effect" of certain highlights in order to achieve luminosity in the flesh.[103] Thus, on the one hand the artist was most receptive to those aspects of nature (his "dictionary") which suited his artistic needs, while on the other hand he sought to justify his decorative color harmonies by touches of naturalistic lighting, and to ground his fantasies in realistic details.

Delacroix used larger areas of intense color in the *Jacob* than in the *Heliodorus* and with a profoundly dramatic expressiveness: the sky glows with ruddy heat on the warm flesh both of the wrestlers and of the figures in the briskly marching caravan—the warmest colors, indeed, are human and animal; Delacroix's forest has a refreshingly green or pearly-gray color, and the distant mountains—not the glowing sky!—are a cool blue. If this "feast for the eye" leads to compositional unity, it does so by its consistent richness and variety rather than by the more controlled repetition of colors, as in the *Heliodorus*. By spotting vivid colors amidst large, relatively neutralized areas, Delacroix enriched his painting without causing disharmony. Touches of dull orange, the muted complement of green, placed in the clump of dark grass, intensify the green without disturbing the integrity of the area. Similarly, outside the green areas broad streams of luminous color (umber-greens and faded oranges) flow, interrupted here and there by intensely colored spots like sparkling islands. In his method of enriching the color of the grass by multiplying the nuances of green in it, Delacroix applied a lesson he had learned from Constable.[104]

As in the *Heliodorus*, reflections in the landscape not only enliven what might otherwise have seemed like studio lighting, and enrich the color, but aid the composition by interlocking contiguous areas: the edge of Jacob's knee seems to melt into the angel's cloak through the reflected

palettes de Delacroix," in *Le Musée de Montpellier*, Paris, 1876, 375-76. Ever since Alberti and Leonardo such generalizations have been made and contested. C. R. Leslie (1794-1859), whom Delacroix knew and admired, in his note to the *Memoirs of ... John Constable*, 334, criticized "the unfounded aphorisms ... as that *shadow is colourless*, that *lights should be warm and shadows cool* or *shadows warm and lights cool*, etc.... [the young artist's] eye will soon perceive

that the tones both of light and shadow are infinitely varied according to circumstances; that ... reflection and refraction change more or less every colour...."

102. See the *Journal*, January 13, 1857. Cf. Leslie, *loc. cit.*

103. See the *Journal*, January 1, 1861, referring to an older entry of October 11, 1852 which discussed Rubens' *Kermesse*.

104. See *Journal*, September 23, ca. 1846.

red dots appearing in both of them; throughout the areas of orange-brown skin, spots of reflected green or greenish gray link the wrestlers to the grass around them; and traces of warm color reflected on the surface of the water (much clearer in the Vienna sketch) link the water to the land. It has already been pointed out that Delacroix was in the vanguard of those Romantics who began to look outside their studio windows. In the wrestlers he tried to realize his observation that the "true color" of flesh is to be found under sunlight in the open air.[105] Compared to the *Heliodorus*, the *Jacob* has many less polished and reflective surfaces; however, landscape admits a greater range than architecture of plausible variation in its color; and Delacroix fully used this range.

The still life of the *Jacob* contains two good examples based on the method of reflected color: the white scarf and the yellow hat. Decoratively the scarf acts as an enlarged "highlight" for the whole group, and especially as a bright foil to bring out the deep blue of the mantle. On the other hand, the "whiteness" of the scarf is nowhere pure but changes with the neighboring colors to a variety of off-whites. Where the scarf overlaps the orange-brown spear on the side toward the spearhead, there is a deep purple shadow; the half-light is a pale gray-green; and the highlight (reflecting perhaps the yellow hat nearby) is a pale yellow. The straw hat, a superbly conceived finishing touch, like the golden objects in the *Heliodorus* brightens the foreground with its strong yellow highlights and a local color tending toward orange, both colors intensified by the contrast with its half-tones of gray-green reflected from the neighboring grass and with shadows which vary from siena to purple.[106]

b) The Relation of Color to Luminosity and Brush Stroke

In decorating the walls of Saint-Sulpice, Delacroix faced once more a long-standing problem (one which the Venetian masters had already coped with) of the greatest importance to him: to produce as light a painting as possible in order to compensate for the inadequate lighting of the

---

105. See *Journal*, September 7, 1856, and January 23, 1857.
106. An insight into the significance of the yellow can perhaps be gleaned from the book by Delacroix's friend, Mme. Elisabeth Cavé, *Le dessin sans maître*, Paris, 1850, for which he wrote an enthusiastic review in *Revue des deux mondes*, 7, 1850. In her "7th Letter" Mme. Cavé wrote: "Have you observed how a straw hat always gives the finishing touch to the toilette? The reason of it is simple enough: nearly all flowers have a little yellow; hence, yellow, like green, produces a good effect with all the other colors."
107. See *Journal*, September 29, 1850.
108. See Sérullaz, *Les peintures*, 60. On the growing tendency to lighten the palette after 1830, see Rosenthal, *Du romantisme*, 293.
109. Delacroix tried his hand at the luminous technique of true fresco in the murals of Valmont in 1834, probably with his commission for the Salon du Roi of the Palais Bourbon (1833-38) in mind. He felt that the technique had certain advantages, as he wrote to Villot in October 1834: "You are right, my nature seems ill-fitted to the colored cartoon—so much for disadvantages. But now as to the advantages: the obligation to do everything at once excites the mind quite differently from the slow process of oil painting. Besides, my greatest misfortune has always been to retouch what was hit on at the first attempt."

chapel, without thereby weakening the color. In his own words: "Making the light and the breadth of the planes dominate too much leads to the absence of half-tones and consequently to lack of coloring; the opposite abuse is harmful above all in large compositions destined to be seen from afar, like ceilings, etc. In the latter kind of painting, Paul Veronese surpasses Rubens through the simplicity of his local color and his breadth in treating the light....Veronese had to intensify his local color greatly so that it would not look colorless when illuminated by the broad light he threw on it."[107] This problem was of particular importance to him, since he had been publicly criticized in 1843 for painting too darkly while decorating the library of the Palais Bourbon.[108] Having earlier experimented (in 1834) with fresco, which did not suit him, the artist had returned to an oil medium.[109] However, another problem connected with the visibility of big murals resulted from the glossy surfaces produced by oil media, *viz.*, the difficulty to see the painting from certain angles. These considerations led Delacroix to mix oil with wax (a mat medium that he preferred, as we have seen, also for its permanence); [110] to introduce a middle tone (half-tone) of light gray as a background; and finally, to prepare a special palette which served for Saint-Sulpice and for most of his paintings of 1850-1863. For this palette Delacroix selected 27 different colors besides 23 combinations of those colors. Of the latter 19 contained white, and only one (gray) contained black, which was replaced by browns or mixtures of complementaries. In order to ensure optimal harmonies, he kept color notes—as he had done for his earlier murals—on little strips of canvas, indicating which colors could best be combined for the light and shadow, half-tone and reflection.[111]

The most extensive and obvious means employed in the *Heliodorus* to unify its tonality is the light-gray architecture, which serves as a foil for the flesh tones of the figures. Delacroix had observed in the Venetians as well as in Rubens that a light half-tone, applied all over the painting and serving as a base on which to add the highlights and shadows of details such as the flesh, allowed a facility and vivacity of execution that were lacking when these details were

In his later references to true fresco, the artist became much more critical of the technique. He did not repeat the experiment of Valmont in his large murals, and continued to rely mainly on oil.

110. On the question of matness, see Villot, *Catalogue de la vente...Delacroix*, and Rosenthal, *Du romantisme*, 329. Lassalle-Bordes, in vol. II of Burty's second edition of Delacroix's letters, Paris, Charpentier, 1880 (2 vols.), made remarks pertinent to the question of the artist's struggle to find a "means to provide light and transparency in a place lacking light" in the Salon du Roi of 1833-37. Contemporary stage designers, it may be noted, faced a similar problem until the inven-

tion first of gas and then of electric lighting helped solve it. Cf. Rosenthal, *Du romantisme*, 104. For discussion of the medium with regard to permanence, see above, the introduction to Chapter II.

111. For the palettes, see Andrieu, "Les palettes de Delacroix," *Le Musée de Montpellier*, 361-76. In the sheer multitude of his colors for the chapel decorations, Delacroix went far beyond the simpler palettes of Rubens and Van Dyck, which form the core of his own. Later artists—perhaps excepting Gustave Moreau—required far fewer colors than Delacroix, but they profited from his lush palette in having a wider choice of colors available. Signac, in his *D'Eugène Delacroix au*

painted in isolation.[112] The artist regarded the painting of flesh as very important for colorists and noted the need for it "in modern subjects, which present little nudity."[113] In the *Heliodorus* flesh tones are exploited for color effects by deliberately exposing the limbs of the important figures in the foreground, whereas the arms and legs of those in the background are more completely covered or of a dark coloration. Here again, there is an intermingling of realistic and decorative intentions; for Delacroix felt that the prominent figures, by receiving strong, direct sunlight, would show their "true color," while he also required the brightness and warmth of flesh as a strong color opposition to the gray architecture.[114]

Delacroix's brush stroke—its thickness and thinness, its roughness and smoothness—is closely related to his color techniques. Just as he opened certain edges of objects to help link them to their neighbors, so he applied brush strokes thinly or discontinuously at the edges to help link one color mass to another; on the other hand, he placed thick, rough-textured strokes over smooth areas to enliven them or to emphasize their significance.

The great variety of brush strokes in the *Heliodorus* can be studied in several examples: the gold bowl (between the gray platter and the box in the corner), whose edges, passing from highlight to shadow, disappear at some points; the lake and vermilion ribbon in the corner with the rapidly applied, thick strokes of paint at its center and with the varied smears and spots on its margins; and the inside contour of the left arm of the girl running upstairs, which dissolves into a blue-gray shadow, its "contour" being suggested by the edges where lights and shadows touch. In general, through the interplay of the edge and the color mass of the forms, Delacroix often tried to avoid the hard contours which Ingres preferred, and explicitly instructed his pupil De Planet to leave a neutral "*fond*" as the "air" around objects, in place of contours.[115]

Some of the most exciting passages throughout the *Jacob* depend also on Delacroix's masterful touch as in the river, painted with parallel, horizontal and nearly straight strokes in contrast to the diversified, often curving strokes of the bank or in the clump of greenery behind Jacob, composed of free irregular strokes. The flowers at the base of the central tree are enlivened by a

---

néo-impressionnisme, ch. iii, overemphasized the simplification of Delacroix's palette. Degas, for example, fascinated by Delacroix's color, tried to adopt his palette, but gave it up as unwieldy. See Denis Rouart, *Degas à la recherche de sa technique*, Paris, 1945, 46. The tendency to simplify the palette was under way earlier, and was advised even by some of Delacroix's contemporaries among the academic painters such as Couture and the slightly later Gérôme! On the former, see *Thomas Couture (1815-79). Sa vie, son oeuvre*, 118; on the latter, see Georges Rivière, *Renoir et ses amis*, Paris, 1921, 54. Desiring at the same time sensuous colors and solidity of form, Dela-

croix achieves both through a large palette: he could produce a great variety of unusual colors adapted to his exotic subjects, and he could surround each new local color with its appropriate half-tone, reflection and shadow. The Impressionists, aiming at a more precise rendering of colors in nature, would seem to require a large palette; but they actually were not hampered by a smaller one than Delacroix's, since they attempted to capture effects within a very narrow range for individual paintings.

112. In the *Journal* on October 5, 1847, after speaking of the Venetian and Flemish use of white grounds, he commented that "the backgrounds and drap-

variety of touches: the smoothness of the dull green regions where the strokes blend; the thick strokes of light gray-green apparently applied slowly; the thin, swift strokes of bright green; the dabs of yellowish white; the long soft finger-like strokes in the deep purple shadows; and the thick strokes of the ochre, sienna and orange highlights. An interplay of line and texture similar to that of the *Heliodorus* activates many forms: the contours of the hill and the tree trunk are interrupted by the brush stroke; the band shape of the scarf is splintered, and its ends frayed out; and the convoluted folds of the blue cloak are built up out of many hatchings.

The importance of these methods for Delacroix's mural decorations was pointed out by Fréd-éric Villot, who noted that the artist, using a technique he called *flochetage*, emphasized the ensemble by interlacing and blending his colors rather than by setting them down obviously and with brio as he had done in works earlier than the Palais Bourbon project of 1833-1835.[116] The consistent use of *flochetage* would have meant entirely dispensing with the impasto lights and thinned shadows of normal academic practice; in fact, however, the latter practice is used in many places, such as in the wings of the angels of both paintings.[117] With ordinary chiaro-scuro effects employing impasto for the lights, the viewer can distinguish the forms within a considerable range, whereas with *flochetage* he requires a distance sufficient for the colors to blend into meaningful patterns. Delacroix's technique can best be understood by the thorough analysis of an example. I have therefore chosen a detail from the lower edge of the *Heliodorus* (a similar example could have been found in the *Jacob*) significantly accessible to all spectators, and painted with such exceptional richness as surely to have been executed by the master rather than by the helpers (see color frontispiece).

The golden jewel box embellished with pearls and gems below Heliodorus, whose "pictorial splendor" Paul Signac admired,[118] merits detailed study. I have chosen to discuss the pearls in particular, for they are a class of similar objects which look different depending on the light. Furthermore, grouped together they strikingly resemble Titian's famous bunch of grapes, which the great colorist painted not as separate forms but fused into masses of light and shadow.

eries...have their share in the painting of flesh, when one executes them with glazes on white grounds." Also see the *Journal*, January 13, 1857.

113. See the *Journal*, January 13, 1857.

114. Cases in which the background seems lighter and more intense than the figures before it also occur and depend on a different consideration, *viz.*, that surrounding the figures are regions darker than the backgrounds, such as hair. In the *Journal* on March 14, 1858 Delacroix wrote: "The most general rule is always to have back-grounds with a bright half-tone, less bright than the flesh, of course, but conceived so that the dark accessories such as the clothing, beard, hair make a dark contrast to bring out the ob-jects of the foreground." The figures in the back-ground on the balcony and landing exhibit this rule clearly, as does the large central red drapery whose dark-red and purple right margin is set off by the light background wall behind it, while its left edge is highlighted in yellow.

115. See De Planet, *Souvenirs*, 97.

116. See Villot, *Catalogue de la vente...Delacroix*, February 11.

117. Delacroix criticized this practice, which is found even in Rubens, as academic, in the *Journal*, III, 380 n.d.

118. See Paul Signac, "Le sujet en peinture," *Encyclo-*

Delacroix certainly knew of this either from fellow artists or from one of the many sources referring to it, perhaps Reynold's *Essay on Fresnoy*, or his follower John Burnet's *Essay on the Education of the Eye* (1837), both of which he had probably read. Thus, one of the most impressive passages of the whole painting may provide a link in the long chain of colorists extending from the Venetian Renaissance to Neo-Impressionism.

An instructive comparison can be made between two of the pearls spilled from the jewel box. One of them, in the light, has a highlight of very bright, warm yellow, whereas the other, in the shadow, has a highlight of pale blue coming from the pervasive blue light of the sky. The pearl in the light has a local color of dull, pale yellow, a half-tone of pale blue and a shadow of dark purple-brown. The yellow highlight looks "natural," since it can be accounted for either by the direct sunlight or by the light reflected from the golden jewel box beside it. But is it also natural to make the local color of a pearl yellow instead of the more characteristic gray? The answer seems to be that once more Delacroix used color not wholly for verisimilitude but as an element of the composition. By extending the yellow color of the highlight to the local color, he ensured that the pearl would not be a speck swallowed up in the dominant purple shadows, but on the contrary would emerge as a luminous form.[119]

The pearl in the shadow has a local color of dull orange, a half-tone of dull green and a shadow of purplish brown, darker and more intense than the shadow of the pearl in the light. Since it is placed beside an orange local color, the blue-tinted highlight emerges clearly and detaches from the body of the pearl, while the rest of the pearl merges in the purple shadows. The orange local color, advancing from the purple shadow, meets the complementary blue highlight, with the result that it is rendered gray by contrast. Similarly, on the pearl in the light, the more intense warm yellow of the highlight drives the duller yellow local color toward gray. What is achieved, then, is an effect of pearly gray without actually using gray, a result corresponding to a fusion of interlaced brush strokes when seen at a distance.

Not all the pearls resemble the two chosen for discussion; in fact, some lack highlights and others are surrounded by shadows made of a cool glaze over a warm dark-purple undertone. These shadows make the individual pearls seem more luminous and coherent by contrast with the paler local color. Many pearls have an orange glow, which is surprising since most of them have no more than a few tiny spots of orange. I believe that this glow derives from the enhancement of the spots of orange by contrast with the deep purple shadows within the group of

pédie française, 1935, XVI, ch. ii, 3. I have quoted from Françoise Cachin's volume, *Paul Signac*, in the series "Miroirs de l'art," 1964, 155, where *coffret* is misprinted *coffet*.

119. For another example—already mentioned—of how Delacroix preferred a color for its decorative rather than for its "natural" effect, see *Journal*, January 1, 1861.

120. Similar observations can be made about other objects in the painting, such as the jewel box between the orange bowl and the gold vase in

pearls and with the cooler gray of the stairs. On the other hand, the pearl gray is sustained by an ingenious spotting of green, blue and red gems of relatively intense coloring. This dual quality depends on the viewer's distance from the painting: seen close up, the great variety of treatment of hue and intensity appears with palpable distinctness. When the pearls are seen from far enough away to lose distinctness, they become part of a larger unit including the darker and cooler stairs, and seem colored a light gray tinged with orange. At such a distance the pearls take their place as an object playing a role in the larger drama of the whole painting.[120]

In this chapter we have explored the complexity of the paintings at Saint-Sulpice as an interplay between broad artistic traditions and the artist's personality. The analysis has shown that tensions between the form and color resulted from contrary tendencies within the artist's style. In the next chapter, through a discussion of the criticism of the paintings, we shall see how these qualities affected Delacroix's contemporaries.

the lower left corner, whose rich coloring and interlaced brush strokes blend at a distance into a solidly cubic form. Some of Delacroix's contemporaries, anticipating the attitude of the Impressionists, emphasized the importance of distance as a factor in viewing paintings. See Horner, *Baudelaire*, 87. William I. Homer, *Seurat and the Science of Painting*, Cambridge, 1964, 167-70 (and notes), cites the opinions of Seurat's contemporaries on this question.

IV. THE CRITICISM OF THE MURALS

Delacroix's contemporaries greeted the opening of his chapel with such intensive discussion that more criticism of it was published than of any other of his mural decorations.[1] The range of responses—from admiration to abhorrence—was by no means unusual for an artist whose work had from the outset been the center of passionate critical debates: the qualities which some had called brutal and naive in his youth, and others powerful and original, were now in his old age called decadent and senile by some, and subtle and masterly by others.[2] With regard to the chapel there recurred the question of Delacroix's modernity (defined vaguely, but usually with reference to his self-expression and color), which hostile critics regarded as a sign of decadence or presumption (Lavergne, Galichon, Cantaloube), and which friendly critics (Brès, Baudelaire) regarded as a sign of his genius. While by 1861 some of the old vocabulary of abuse—"a real mess," "butcheries," "barbarous disregard for conventions," "disturbed imagination"—were less conspicuous than more tepid perennials such as "careless drawing" and "sketchiness," certain notes sounding beneath the tedious clichés (favorable as well as unfavorable) indicate that the criticism marked some profoundly important issues not only of religious painting but of advanced art.

The central questions with regard to the religious aspect of the decorations were whether a powerful artistic expression by a living artist was consistent with the role of painting as moralizing and didactic, and whether a great artist without faith could produce religious painting of high quality. Actually, for most Catholic critics of the nineteenth century the two questions were closely linked, inasmuch as faith no longer meant passionate belief but adherence to tradition and moralizing acquiescence in dogmas; hence the prejudice of such writers as Lavergne, Duplessis, Gruyer, Merson, and Boissard, who were repelled by Delacroix's dramatic paintings, seeing in them only an occasion for faultfinding, especially with his lack of finish and his "incorrect drawing." In general Catholic critics of religious art at this time tended to associate color, movement and "ugliness" (meaning either the homely or the unduly expressive) with materi-

1. For an arrangement of excerpts from this criticism in their order of publication, and information about the critics, see Appendix III.
2. For a selection of criticism from all periods of Delacroix's career, see Tourneux, *Delacroix devant ses contemporains*; Horner, *Baudelaire*; and Sérullaz, *Les peintures*.
3. Merson in the *Revue contemporaine*, March 15, 1862, 152-67, and A. Gruyer in his book *Essai sur les fresques de Raphael au Vatican*, Paris, 1863, 187-97, both severe critics of Delacroix, admired the calm, devout isolation of Raphael's Onias, and the remarkable empty space in the center of the painting, which focuses attention on the praying High Priest. Gruyer explained that "the absolute emptiness in the middle of the fresco divides the people into two distinct groups, adds to the moral unity of the subject, and gives to the drama its spontaneity and irresistible movement." It is noteworthy that Ingres himself, writing in 1814, found just this element of the composition praiseworthy: "In the *Heliodorus* he has placed, as is his custom (and it is fine), the principal groups around the edges and has left an empty space in the middle." The remark is quoted in Ingres, *Ecrits sur l'art: Textes recueillis dans les carnets et dans la correspondance de Ingres*, Preface by Raymond Cogniat, La Jeune Parque, n.d., 44. For a discussion of "the aesthetics of emptiness" as a factor in western

ality, and line, repose and beauty with spirituality. By comparing Delacroix to Raphael or to the pre-Raphaelites in order to expose his presumed inadequacies as a mural decorator, and to demonstrate that his quest for originality had led him to the "ugly," they approached the position of Ingres.[3] Curiously, their standpoint combined Catholic sympathies with an approach to art whose academic language ("unity," "logic," "beauty" vs. "ugliness," and "soul" vs. "sense") and didactic outlook came out of the anticlerical tradition of Davidian classicism. Opposed to these critics (and there was no significant middle ground between the two) were those who appreciated the paintings from an artistic point of view (Gautier, Baudelaire, Brès, Bernard) and who, while not praising them as examples of Christian art, attributed to them a moral or spiritual value arising from the artist's passion and sincerity. Delacroix's admirers applied the whole vocabulary of praise which had passed from the Rubenist De Piles to the Romantics: genius, spontaneity, expressive line, color and modernism.

The importance of these debates was to call attention to the current crisis in church decoration and to clarify its causes by indicating a deep split between the aesthetic and religious viewpoints and by demonstrating the irrelevance of orthodox belief to high quality in religious painting.[4] The suggestions of some critics that religious art could be rejuvenated if new themes were invented, or if old ones like biblical landscapes and Oriental subjects were cultivated, were pointless without good artists to realize them.[5]

The *Heliodorus* provoked the most comment among Catholics, probably in part owing to a topical interest in its theme; for recent aggressions against the Church, supported by Napoleon III, had aroused the hostility of French Catholics toward the Emperor.[6] Among the Catholic critics only Lavergne made explicit reference to the moral that any aggressor who, like Heliodorus, "outraged the Tiara and the Cross" would be "blasted with divine blows." However, he found this idea illustrated not by Delacroix's painting but by Raphael's, where the Pope is included among the characters. If the frequent references to the Vatican fresco—and the regrets

art, see C. Gilbert, "On Subject and Non-Subject in Italian Renaissance Pictures," *AB*, 24, 1952, 202-16.

4. Castagnary, an atheist, wrote that "religious painting has disappeared from the Salon," but the low quality of religious painting in 1861 was even admitted by apologists of Christian art such as F. Beslay, who in his Salon of that year, published in the *Revue d'économie chrétienne*, Paris, 490-514, lamented that "the immortal themes of great painting inspire today only artists without talent and without faith, judging by their works." Aside from the isolated case of Puvis de Chavannes, not until the 20th century was there to be a revival of great church decoration, and by men

who were often skeptics or even atheists. On the 20th century revival see, e.g., Rubin, *Modern Sacred Art and the Church of Assy*.

5. Such proposals were put forward by Gustave Planche in "La peinture murale," *Revue des deux mondes*, 6, 1856, 44-75, and F. Beslay, 1861 Salon.

6. Briefly, in 1859 Napoleon III had, by defeating the Austrians in Italy, contributed to the unification of the country under Victor-Emmanuel II, who outraged Catholics by confiscating most of the states of the Church in 1860, and who proclaimed himself King of Italy in March 1861, several months before the opening of Delacroix's chapel. Ironically, the French state, which had helped bring about a disaster to the Church, had

accompanying them that the later version was a personal statement without religious or moral value—contained a veiled criticism of Napoleon III, then it must be admitted that the criticism was so vague as to be ineffectual.

The impotence of the Catholic critics is not surprising, under the conditions prevailing in Napoleon III's Empire, which in its efforts to squelch disaffection, liberal or otherwise, had rigorously censored all publications. Ambitious to emulate his great model Napoleon I, the Emperor regarded Delacroix not so much as a courageously independent artist but as a famous painter quite unconcerned with dangerous political questions who, like Ingres, could shed glory on the Second Empire. Louis Bonaparte's clever and successful opportunism (which led him in 1851 to support the Church, and in 1861 to oppose it while granting concessions to the liberals) characterized a political situation which induced among French intellectuals and artists, who had hoped for so much in 1848, a profound disillusion and an indifference to politics. Interesting exceptions were those ardent republicans who had quit government posts to protest the Emperor's seizure of power, and who criticized aspects of the State's activities as expressions of their otherwise muted hostility; could this help explain why Charles Blanc, once sympathetic to Delacroix's art, revealed such curiously mixed feelings toward the artist's state-supported mural decorations?[7]

In order to understand why so much of the public interested in art was drawn into controversies over a chapel decoration at a time when critics—sympathetic and unsympathetic to Catholicism alike—noted the decline of religious painting in France, the discussions must be considered not only as concerning the work of a famous artist, but in relation to the repressiveness of the Second Empire.[8] In such a climate the energies of the public were diverted from issues of politics to those of art and religion, where one could talk with less restraint; and as romantic liberalism fell into political apathy, it was replaced by "art for art's sake." In fact, the debates over the murals meant to Napoleon III no more than a politically innocuous though noisy tribute to the artist, whatever it may have meant to Delacroix and his public. Liberal bourgeois critics like Gustave Planche, unhappy but unprotesting, in their criticism no longer touched political issues, and the artists themselves no longer felt impelled to treat themes with a provocative social content.[9] The old association of the politically revolutionary with the artistically "modern" was in this period broken.

also paid for this painting, whose subject embodied a pro-Vatican message, since the import of the story of Heliodorus ever since Raphael made it famous was that the Pope always triumphs over his enemies on earth.

7. Louis Vitet, like Blanc, was a disaffected republican, whose criticism of the murals was ambivalent (Vitet's earlier critique of Delacroix's *Marino Faliero* in 1827 also had opposed judg-

ments). See Appendix III.

8. On the decline of religious painting see the Catholic critic Beslay, 1861 Salon, and the anticlerical critics Thoré and Castagnary. Cf. note 4, above.

9. On Planche, see Pontus Grate, "Deux critiques d'art de l'époque romantique," *Figura*, 12, 1959. Clearly, there was no occasion now to inspire such works as the *Oath of the Horatii* (1784), the

This abandonment of great revolutionary themes is a later phase of a process already under way at the end of the eighteenth century, wherein the grandiose themes of history and religious painting gradually disappeared. Despite Napoleon III's efforts to sustain it by monumental commissions, the academic tradition of *grand art*, long in decline, was about to fall completely.[10] Thoré wrote in 1847 that "the subject is absolutely indifferent in the arts," and by 1866 Zola could admire both Delacroix and Courbet, beyond their different subject matter, as examples of well-defined "temperament."

The issue of *grand art* was sharply focused in the criticism of the paintings at Saint-Sulpice, the last important examples of the genre. Baudelaire, the most sensitive appreciator of the decorations, while certainly aware of their attachment to an obsolete tradition, artfully divorced color from subject matter and, ignoring Delacroix's zealous researches as well as the excitement of other contemporaries over his archaeology, wrote: "...when you come closer and analyze the subject, nothing will be deducted from or added to, that original pleasure [in the color], for its source lies elsewhere and far away from any material thought."

This emphasis on the pleasure to be felt in the presence of Delacroix's murals touched on the widely discussed question of whether pure pleasure, without moral, religious or other extra-artistic content was an adequate goal for art, or could lead to good art. The new importance given to the spectator's pleasure and to the artist's personal expression signified the end of the long debate over *grand art*, and when Delacroix, adopting a phrase current in the 1850's, wrote two months before his death that "the first merit of painting is to be a feast for the eye," he was stating a view coming to be held by increasing numbers of young artists. These issues—mainly implicit in the discussions of Delacroix's murals—characterize a moment in the history of French art on the threshold of the *Salon des Refusés* of 1863.

Raft of the Medusa (1819), the *Liberty on the Barricades* (1830), or the *Stone Breakers* (1849); but new attitudes to subject matter also influenced the aversion to great social themes. Cf. Rosenthal, *Du romantisme*, 320.

10. Thoré's remark, with regard to the chapel decorations, that "great art is not absolutely lost in France," was a compliment to Delacroix's exceptional quality, not a denial of the critic's thesis about the obsolescence of the genre. Henri Lehmann, in his article "Porche de Saint-Germain-l'Auxerrois. Fresques de M. Victor Mottez," *L'artiste*, November 8, 1846, 1, attributed "the failure since 1834" to produce great monumental painting to the immodest attitude of the young, who preferred a premature assertion of their personality to disciplined cooperation with masters on big projects.

At Saint-Sulpice Delacroix was able to revitalize the tired tradition of *grand art* because he himself identified with grandeur and because the conventional symbolism of his subjects held for him overtones of personal significance. Viewing religious subjects as artistic challenges rather than as an expression of orthodox religious belief, he accepted from the French state this commission for a church decoration as eagerly as he had others for government buildings such as the city hall of Paris or the Louvre. He tackled all of these large projects despite the disappearance of important mural painting techniques and the loss of a workshop tradition common in the Renaissance, realizing his ideas in a protracted collaboration with helpers whom he in part trained and whose work he guided. Big mural paintings—as opposed to smaller and less permanent easel paintings—were a passion with the artist, who wrote that his "heart beats faster in the presence of large walls to paint."[1]

In this quest for grandeur, the Romantic emulated old masters such as Raphael, Titian and Rubens, whose subjects or styles so much affected his work on the chapel decorations; indeed, even in his youth, when someone linked him to the then-vigorous movement of romanticism and to its leader Hugo, he objected with the famous reply: "You are mistaken, sir, I am a pure classic." The complex motivations which drew him back to tradition (finding—like Reynolds—in antiquity and the Renaissance the sources of modern art) and forward to his contemporaries, have become clear from our examination of the sketches, which revealed a range extending from loose and impulsive gesture-drawings to precise and superbly rendered studies of detail. The difficulties resulting from these apparently incompatible qualities were often noticed by critics writing about the chapel decorations after the end of the nineteenth century, who found aspects of both romanticism and classicism in them.[2] Even Delacroix's exoticism was a reaction against a confining classicism; thus, his remark with reference to the "classical" mien and dress of the

1. See the *Journal*, June 30, 1854. For a discussion, with brief bibliography, of the relation of large scale to "the grand style" in the Renaissance, see Webster Smith, "Giulio Clovio and the 'Maniera di Figure Piccole,'" *AB*, 46, 1964, 395-401, passim, esp. n. 14.

2. Meier-Graefe, in *Modern Art*, II, 152, considered the Raphaelesque drapery in Delacroix's *Heliodorus* a minor flaw in a painting admirable for its color, and raised the question of the Romantic Delacroix's ability to paint large murals: "He composed to some extent in sections, in long-drawn gasps....This is evident in all his great decorations." W. Friedländer, *David to Delacroix*, Harvard, 1952, 129, distinguished between the artist's traditional form in the mural paintings and "the progressive neo-baroque of his color movement." U. Christoffel, *Von Poussin zu Ingres und Delacroix*, Zürich, 1945, 94, maintained that Delacroix's classicism in the *Heliodorus* "approached the style of the David-Ingres tendency." Jacques Feydy, in his article, "Romantisme, classicisme et baroque. Aperçus sur Delacroix," *Revue des sciences humaines*, April-September 1951, 220, asserted that "the origins of the Classic and the Baroque mingle," and described Delacroix's *Heliodorus* as "a Rubenized Raphael." Walter Pach, in *The Classical Tradition in Modern Art*, 43, blurred the dis-

North Africans, "Rome is no longer in Rome," meant both bypassing the routine Davidian "trip to Rome" and snubbing some of the very masterpieces he admired (in engravings) and feared.[3]

Delacroix's involvement with tradition was by no means academic, and he felt a deep personal engagement with the older masters not only in his paintings but in his writings about them; e.g., with regard to the "sublime" quality he felt in the Michelangelesque works of Rubens and Géricault he wrote: "It is probable that the only reason why these works please me so much is that they correspond to feelings which are my own; and since they give me the same degree of pleasure, different as they are, it must be that I find in myself the source of the effect which they produce."[4] Similarly, the grand architecture of the *Heliodorus* meant more to him than a stage setting to be filled out with exotic local color, and the great trees of the *Jacob* display the Romantic's sense of the majesty and power of nature.

While the larger forms and broader color masses in the murals are associated with the tradition of *grand art*, many details which were painted with evident enthusiasm exhibit on close examination a wealth of invention and a richness of coloring and look surprisingly unconventional and fresh; indeed, the fabric of varied brush strokes on such details constitutes a much more intimate signature to the decorations than the coldly monumental letters "DELACROIX" placed at the bottom of the *Heliodorus*. This duality between the large and public and the small and private—like those we have discussed between classicism and romanticism, nature and imagination, form and color, tradition and modernity, and decoration and expression—contribute to the inexhaustible fascination of Delacroix's great chapel decorations for his own time and for later epochs.

tinction between romanticism and classicism not only for Delacroix but for all outstanding artists: "No great work of art can be found devoid of a romantic or classical strain." Bernard Dorival, in his *Les étapes de la peinture française contemporaine*, Paris, 1946, III, 301, quoted Paul Valéry's remark that Delacroix belongs with the masters of the Renaissance, his *Jacob Wrestling with the Angel* being "the last combat of a great humanist style." For a brief survey of opinions about the relation of classic and romantic tendencies in Delacroix, see Mras, *Delacroix's Theory of Art*, esp. the Introduction. The vitality of classicism for earlier Romantics is maintained by Lorenz

Eitner, "Géricault's 'Dying Paris' and the Meaning of His Romantic Classicism," *Master Drawings*, Spring 1963, 21-34, esp. 32.

3. Delacroix made the remark in his letter to A. Jal on June 4, 1832, advising that students be sent to North Africa to learn of antiquity. It is curious to find the same phrase in a different context pronounced by the principal character in Corneille's *Sertorius*, Act III, Sc. II: "...Rome n'est plus dans Rome, elle est toute où je suis." One of the characters in Ponsard's *Charlotte Corday*, 1850, Act II, Sc. III, alludes to Corneille's well-known phrase.

4. See the *Journal*, October 20, 1853.

1836-1842 Victor-Louis-Mottez (1809-97, a pupil of Ingres): porch of Saint-Germain-l'Auxerrois (frescoes, restored 1855)

1840 Martin Drolling (or Drölling, 1786-1851): Saint-Sulpice, La Chapelle de Saint Paul (two frescoes, completed in 1850: *St. Paul before the Areopage* and *The Conversion of St. Paul on the Road to Damascus*

Hippolyte Flandrin (1809-64, a pupil of Ingres): frescoes at Saint Séverin, chapel of Saint John (completed in 1841)

Adolphe Roger (1800-80, a student of Gros): Notre-Dame de Lorette, baptistery

1842 Hippolyte Flandrin: Saint-Germain-des-Prés, sanctuary, completed in 1846

1843 H. Holfeld (1804-72, a student of A. de Pujol): Saint-Jacques-du-Haut-Pas: *St. Philip Presents Nathaniel to Jesus*

Adolphe Roger: Sainte-Elisabeth, *Let the Small Children Come unto Me*

1844 Camille Corot: Saint-Nicolas-du-Chardonnet, *The Baptism of Christ*, completed in 1845

Chassériau: Saint-Merri, Chapelle de Sainte Marie l'Egyptienne, scenes from the life of the saint

Delacroix: Saint-Denis-du-Saint-Sacrement, *Pietà*

1845 François-Joseph Heim (1787-1865): Saint-Sulpice, Chapelle du Purgatoire, *Religion Encourages a Dying Christian, The Effectiveness of*

Prayer for the Dead, The Intercession of Christ and Mary with God the Father

Joseph Guichard (1806-80, a student both of Ingres and Delacroix): Saint-Germain-l'Auxerrois, *Adoration of the Magi*

1846 Friedrich Bouterwek (1806-67, German, student of P. Delaroche): Saint-Jacques-du-Haut-Pas, *The Visitation*

Hippolyte Flandrin: Saint-Germain-des-Prés, choir: *The Last Supper, The Entry into Jerusalem, The Ascent to Calvary*; nave: Old and New Testament scenes side by side (e.g. *Jonah Saved* vs. *The Resurrection*)

Victor-Louis-Mottez: murals at Saint-Séverin, Chapelle de Sainte-Anne and Chapelle de Sainte-Marie

1847 Thomas Couture: Saint Eustache, Chapelle de la Vièrge, three paintings of the Virgin Mary, completed in 1852

1848 Joseph Guichard: Saint Gervais, Chapelle de Saint-Joseph, *Moses Brings Forth Water from the Rock*

1849 Hippolyte Flandrin: Saint-Vincent-de-Paul, frescoes completed in 1853; on the walls of the nave: a procession of saints

1850 Auguste Lebouys (1812-54, a student of P. Delaroche): Saint-Nicolas-du-Chardonnet, Chapelle du Calvaire, *The Descent from the Cross, Christ Rising from the Tomb*

1852 Alexandre Hesse (1806-79, a student of G. Saint-Séverin, Chapelle de Sainte Genev scenes from the life of the saint

1853 Chassériau: Saint-Roch, *St. Philip Diacre, Baptism of the Eunuch of the Queen of Ethi* completed in 1854

Emile Lafon (1817-86, a student of Gros Delaroche): Saint-Sulpice, Chapelle de S. François Xavier, *Resurrection of a Dead F Funeral of the Saint; The Glorification o: Francis*, completed in 1859

1854 Chassériau: Saint-Roch, Chapelle des F Baptismaux; Saint-Philippe-du-Roule, *The D sition*, finished 1856

Isidore Pils (1813-75, a student of Picot): S Eustache, *The Crucifixion*

1856 Hippolyte Flandrin: Saint-Germain-des-F nave, completed in 1861

1859 Auguste Glaize (1807-93, a student of Eu; and Achille Devéria): Saint-Sulpice, Chapell Saint-Jean, *The Martyrdom of St. John; The S Asking His Disciples to Love One Another*

1860 A. de Curzon (1820-95, a student of Drolli Saint-Nicolas-du-Chardonnet, Chapelle du S Coeur

Alexandre Hesse: Saint-Sulpice, Chapelle Saint François de Sales: *The Saint Preachin the Heretics of Chablois; The Delivery of Constitutions to St. Joan of Chantal; The Glo cation of the Holy Bishop*

RECONSTRUCTIONS OF THE TEMPLE OF JERUSALEM FROM THE SEVENTEENTH TO THE NINETEENTH CENTURY

The Temple of Jerusalem constantly appears in classic plays of the seventeenth and eighteenth centuries, usually in stage settings based on classical models. An intensified interest in its reconstruction occurred in the late sixteenth and early seventeenth centuries, perhaps connected with the publication at that time of two great epics on the theme of Jerusalem Delivered, by Tasso and Lope de Vega. Generally, seventeenth century reconstructions were based on the work of the Spanish Jesuit Francisco de Villalpando (died in Toledo, 1561), who believed that the original model of the Temple could be found in Greek architecture.[1] L. C. Sturm's representation in *Sciagraphia Templi Hierosolymitani, ex ipsis SS. Literarum fontibus* (Leipzig, 1694) combined literary sources such as the Vision of Ezekiel and the writings of Flavius Josephus with the models of Villalpando, and possibly the *Arch of Titus*, a recurrent source for Jewish motifs. Sturm's version looks like a Greco-Roman temple with a pediment over an entablature, an arched doorway, and Corinthian capitals. In French painting, we find Simon Vouet's classical temple in *La présentation au temple*, 1641 (Louvre), and Philippe de Champaigne's temple (based on Villalpando's) in his *Crucifixion* of 1674 (Louvre).[2] Between 1692 and 1702 Luca Giordano executed for a church in Madrid *The Building of the Temple of Jerusalem*, a famous series of five sketches based on classical models.

Post-seventeenth century versions of the Temple do not essentially differ from Sturm's. In the eighteenth century Lamy based his attempt to reconstruct this "incunabulum of all the arts" on little more than variations of the older models, or on renewed conjectures about the biblical texts;[3] e.g., his book has a view of the eastern gate of the Temple which shows several flights of steps rising one above the other, probably derived from the reference in Ezekiel to several stories connected by steps.[4]

The eighteenth and nineteenth century French archaeological explorations of the Near East (e.g., Olivier in Persia and Egypt in 1792-98; the Napoleonic expedition to Egypt from 1798 to 1801, with its subsequent publications; Flandin and Coste to Persia, 1840-41; Botta to Assyria, 1842) added little substance to earlier images of the Temple, and the heated debates between Fergusson and Vogüé as to the appearance and size of Solomon's Temple turned quite often on interpretations of the biblical texts. F.-J. Heim's *Destruction de Jérusalem par les Romains*, 1820-24 (Louvre), shows a temple portico bearing palm capitals, clearly based on engravings of Egyptian ruins.

1. See J. Schlosser-Magnino, *La letteratura artistica*, 3rd ed., Florence, 1964, 659. For a bibliography of Villalpando, see R. Wittkower, *Architectural Principles*, London, 1962, 121-22.

2. See A. Blunt, *Art and Architecture in France 1500-1700*, Harmondsworth, 1957, 151 and n. 157; and W. R. Crelly, *The Painting of Simon Vouet*, New Haven, 1962, fig. 75. In the mid-15th century, Jean Fouquet's "The Building of the Temple of Jerusalem," from his "Antiquités judaïques," Paris, Bib. nat. MS. fr. 247, fol. 163 (illustration 55b in John White, *The Birth and Rebirth of Pictorial Space*, London, 1957), shows the Temple as a Gothic cathedral.

3. *De tabernaculo foederis, de sancta civitate Jerusalem, et de templo eius*, Paris, 1720, 1.

4. See Lamy, *De tabernaculo foederis*, Tab. xiii, "Porta orientalis atriorum Israelis." Cf. Ezekiel 40:22-25 and 41:4-7.

While Delacroix's chapel was open to the public only after August 23, 1861, some critics sympathetic to the artist were admitted as early as the end of July 1861. The first published criticism, Théophile Gautier's of August 3, 1861, was published in the *Moniteur universel* (and again on September 1, 1861 in *L'artiste*) and was filled with compliments of these paintings "executed in wax." He said of the *St. Michael*: "This painting of a bright and sumptuous tone makes the vault disappear and makes the chapel look like a hypaethral temple.... This sky of golden and turquoise tones would bear comparison with the sky of Paul Veronese in the *Apotheosis of Venice* in the Ducal Palace." Of the *Heliodorus* he remarked: "This subject has been treated by Raphael with his divine superiority; but the subject is so complex...that one can take up again the theme used by one of the gods of painting without sacrilege, and vary it in one's own manner. What Sanzio understood from the point of view of style, M. Eugène Delacroix envisaged from the point of view of color movement. The two works, aside from all appreciation of their value, in no way resemble one another." He praised Delacroix, "the painter colorist," for the gems and for the great beauty of the light in the *Heliodorus*: "These so marvelously successful plays of color do not detract from the seriousness of the composition and do not at all diminish the moral value." He had less to say of the *Jacob*, noting that it is a triumph to fill a large space with two figures successfully, and that its landscape recalls Titian's in the *Martyrdom of Saint Peter*.

Thoré's article of August 9, 1861, under the pseudonym of W. Bürger,[2] compared Delacroix's long labor to Michelangelo's in the Sistine Chapel. While he admitted that others have treated the same subjects (Raphael's *Heliodorus*, Rembrandt's *Jacob Wrestling with the Angel*), he found Delacroix's work new and vital, filled with invention. "Jewish

architecture is not very familiar to the archaeologists; and here it is restored by a painter's intuition. As M. Delacroix explained the character of his architecture, saying that he had sought to distinguish it from the style of Egypt and Upper Asia, M. Charton, who was there, said, 'Well, well! The magazine *Trip Around the World* has just published a piece of a column, recently discovered in Jerusalem, which has the same character.'[3] Architecture is very important in this composition of the *Heliodorus*." As an approach to Delacroix's genius, Thoré distinguished line, "the framework, the skeleton of art," from color, "its soul," and wherein the artist's charm and originality lies: "Cut off, at random, a square inch in a painting by Delacroix, and you will recognize in it his palette, you will have the pleasure that a bouquet of flowers or a jewel with fine stones gives." In the *Heliodorus*, he praised the "light everywhere, even in the shadows, scurochiaro (*l'obscur clair*)—to reverse the word chiaroscuro—a delicious local color, bold shapes, the great splendor of the whole...." He especially appreciated the *Jacob*, considering it superior to the *Heliodorus*, which has some "imperfections of detail." "In the *Jacob*, we are in open air, and the architecture of landscape has no less preoccupied M. Delacroix than the construction of the Jewish temple.... This nature is in harmony with the architectural style of the *Heliodorus*." Thoré admired Delacroix's achievement of keeping so large a surface interesting with only two figures of appreciable size. "The landscape is dominant...and one of the greatest nature pieces that would ever have been attempted in any School."[4] He found the *St. Michael* least successful of the three paintings. In concluding, he exclaimed: "Great art *(le grand art)* is not absolutely lost in France! Here is monumental painting worthy of the much celebrated ancient frescoes."

Louis Brès's review in the *Moniteur des arts* of

August 31, 1861, rang with enthusiastic praise: "On can only compare it to the works of the old Floren tine or Venetian masters. In the epochs of artist faith, people went with enthusiasm to acclaim th immortal work, but although there are only rar initiates who go piously to admire the master's work the joy is not less great among the devotees of art. He liked the *Heliodorus* best, calling it "the mo seductive of the three compositions." Of the *Jaco* he said: "It is the combat of matter against spiri Admirable glorification of the idea!" *St. Micha* shows "the triumph of good over evil." He con cluded: "The paintings of M. Eugène Delacroix, i the Chapelle des Saints-Anges, will remain one o the greatest pages of modern art and one of th finest claims to glory of the artist...to tell the trut the new paintings may provoke some quite danger ous comparisons!"

On September 15, 1861, Baudelaire's well-know discussion of Saint-Sulpice appeared in the *Revu fantaisiste*, and—in an expanded form—in th *Opinion nationale* on September 2, and Novembe 14 and 22, 1863. It is not necessary to present th full text here, since its essence is readily availabl in Jonathan Mayne's excellent translation, in th *Mirror of Art* (Anchor Book ed., New York, 1956 pp. 306-38. The critic extolled Delacroix's "epi drawing" and his "splendidly and scientificall supernatural color"; emphasized the artist's modern ity founded on his color, which—like a beautifu arabesque—has a vitality independent of subjec matter; and repeated his view that the artist's re ligious painting is a facet of his all-embracing imag ination. An excerpt of this review was include in Baudelaire's homage of 1863 to the recently de ceased artist. It is interesting to note that in dis cussing the paintings of the chapel, the critic omit ted to mention the *St. Michael*, which suggests tha he placed less value on it than on the other tw

---

1. Although about one-third of these texts are now available in Sérullaz, *Les peintures*, this is the first time most have been published in English.
2. Tourneux, *Delacroix devant ses contemporains*, 131, and Joubin, *Correspondance générale*, IV,

269, n. 1, give wrong dates, whereas A. Tabarant, *La vie artistique au temps de Baudelaire*, 3rd ed., Paris, 1942, 514, and Sérullaz, *Les peintures*, 165, give the correct date.
3. On Charton and the illustrations of the columns,

see Chapter III, A, 2.
4. Thoré's preference for the *Jacob* as a landscap and his reference to *plein air* with regard to it ar not accidental; Thoré later sympathized with th Impressionists.

aintings. In a letter of October 8, 1861, thanking audelaire for this eulogistic article, Delacroix spoke f the "mysterious effects of line and color...this usical and arabesque aspect" whose pleasures itics, wanting "to understand in order to be able prove," cannot appreciate.

Following these initial sympathetic reviews, laudius Lavergne, a former student of Ingres, led e assault on Delacroix's paintings in a harshly itical article published in *Le monde* on September and 29, 1861. After taking issue with Théophile autier's acclaim of the artist, Lavergne, while ad- itting Delacroix's inventive genius, censured his religious motives in choosing "dreadful and ani- ated subjects," and in representing angels not as messengers of piety and peace" but as "divine ries." As an example of an association to pagan emes, he pointed to a resemblance between the ontest of St. Michael and the dragon and that of pollo and the Python in Delacroix's decoration at e Louvre. After criticizing the "repulsive ugliness" the angels in the *Heliodorus*, the critic alluded to aphael's Stanze, where the instructive defeats of leliodorus and Attila confront one another: "These nmortal pages...attest that from its beginnings he Church has fought and won its battles and that ach time the combats are renewed, the divine hand ushes the enemy and reestablishes the reign of ustice and peace." Any potential Heliodorus or ttila will learn just by looking at the pictures of aphael "with what divine blows are blasted those vho outrage the Tiara and the Cross." He censured Delacroix's painting for not teaching the same les- on. In the *Jacob* the real subject is the giant trees, or the wrestlers are there only to give scale to the ainting, and only the angel's wings let you know hat a biblical scene is represented. The brush trokes are labored, amateurish hatchings, whereas eal skill would "render the touch and effort in-

visible." The artist's personality is obtrusively pres- ent: "Already one no longer says 'la Chapelle des Saints-Anges' but 'la Chapelle de M. Delacroix.'" Lavergne has discovered that the painting is not true fresco as claimed (he doesn't say by whom), but only "oil painting mixed with wax, just enough to give it the *appearance* of fresco."[5] Curiously, after all this he admitted that Delacroix "is more triumphant than ever," and then he turned sadly to reflect on the fortunes of "that little phalanx of Christian artists which was formed about 1835 in opposition to the romantic school under the auspices of the Comte de Montalembert and M. Rio." He appealed to Delacroix to desist from undermining Christian art: "Belief in the Guardian Angel is popular. Why do you wish to deprive the Catholic democracy of this serene and consoling image?...M. Chenavard has frankly undertaken the reform of clerical super- stitions. M. Delacroix is satisfied to take no account of them." Finally, as a sign of Delacroix's "question- able genius," he pointed to his lack of modesty in painting the chapel, "since MM. H. Vernet, Ary Scheffer, Paul Delaroche and even M. Ingres have constantly refused" to decorate a church.[6]

Delacroix followed with interest the articles as they appeared, and in his letter of October 17, 1861, he told Andrieu: "I don't know where the chapel stands: I've seen few articles. There were some very favorable ones and others rather less friendly."

In the December 1, 1861 issue of the *Gazette des Beaux-Arts*, Galichon's long critique appeared with the editor Charles Blanc's approval.[7] He dwelled as much on general questions of mural and religious painting as on the chapel itself: "The substitution of mural painting for painting on canvas in our monuments is one of the innovations for which true art lovers owe the government and the City of Paris the greatest thanks. Fresco, by allowing neither con- cealments nor subterfuges of touch or color that

mask ignorance, forces the artist to long and con- scientious studies." Church murals must adhere to the great tradition of religious mural painting (Giotto, Orcagna, Fra Angelico, Masaccio) in which the figures drawn have a severe grace, a touching simplicity, a pure and penetrating sentiment, in order that all who look at their works may feel moved and conceive a great and respectful idea of the divinity. "All these masters [Giotto etc.] have come from Florence,...[they] wish to address the soul rather than the senses." Ever since the Greeks and Romans a distinction between the modes of painting has been recognized, and the ancients pre- ferred line and form, the moderns color, "more pleasant at first sight." For a long time some modern artists, wanting to surpass their forerunners, have discarded the laws of mural painting and have "be- lieved themselves able to make up for the want of true beauty by richness, and instead of judging their works from the religious and architectural point of view, criticism is supposed to consider them in iso- lation and analyze them by themselves, as if they were pure paintings, detached from the wall." Thus Eugène Delacroix "has sought in sacred history only some tumultuous scenes that allow him to trace flamboyant lines, strained postures.... If M. Dela- croix, in his paintings, has shown all the fine quali- ties of invention, passion and color that we know him for, he has also let us see the inadequacy of his drawing, the little concern he has for beauty, and his constant preoccupation to seek character in a certain barbarism of expression and modeling which has at least the merit of an incisive originality." Delacroix's figures are ugly but never banal, al- though the "*St. Michael* lacks boldness," since the figures, instead of being foreshortened, are placed horizontally, "giving them a point of support on earth rather than launching them into space." How- ever, this painting, the least successful of the three,

5. The word *fresque* was used in two senses, to mean any technique of painting on walls, as pointed out in the Introduction, note 4, or to refer specifically to the technique of painting on fresh plaster, as practiced by the much-admired High Renaissance masters and therefore vener- ated by the *Ingristes*.

6. Ingres's motives, as well as those of other artists, in refusing, raise a very interesting problem to investigate.

7. Blanc, who had written high praise of Delacroix's religious painting in 1845, stated that Galichon's review "judiciously appreciated" the murals. See *GBA*, 1st ser., 16, 1864, 122; and Blanc, *Les artistes de mon temps*, Paris, 1876, 80 n. 1.

has the merit of color, making the vault disappear and the chapel become hypaethral "according to the words of Théophile Gautier." Its color is found also in the *Heliodorus*, "but with less harmony and unity. The jewels, the vases spread out on the temple steps, the sumptuous materials which cover the envoy of Seleucus, the brilliant armor of the angel of the Lord, are the work of a colorist who knows all the richness, all the secrets of the palette...but one regrets meeting here in place of the general harmony that catches the attention, a scattering that disquiets and dazzles one." There is not enough air in the foreground, "where the persons in action seem to adhere one to the other"; but one should praise "the skill with which he has cast interest into the whole composition." His rich architecture gives a good idea of "the Temple of Jerusalem, whose colossal dimensions spoke so strongly to the imagination of the people....He has ingeniously united this scene of terror and surprise with the drama of punishment, through the figure of the woman mounting the staircase and through that of the angel who with head lowered charges down at Heliodorus." In the *Jacob* he admired "the beautiful landscape with its rustic and Oriental beauty...the magnificence of the view ...all this holds and charms the attention....The long caravan brings us back to those primitive ages when the patriarch wandered in an immense and solitary nature." In sum, he felt that although Delacroix had painted with richness of imagination and "a certain quite modern lyricism, with understanding of the general effect and harmonious color," he had "not satisfied either the laws of religious painting or the conditions of monumental painting."[8]

Ernest Chesneau, writing on "the modern movement in painting" in the *Revue européenne* (which he edited) of December 1861, discussed Delacroix in general, and the "recently opened" chapel in particular: "We impatiently awaited from M. Delacroix

this trial by fresco...a cold process. The artist has remained master." He criticized the *St. Michael*, however, for having too much space with too small figures, and a conventional demon "despite his gold crown." As to the laws of mural painting, requiring a degree of decorative flatness, Delacroix has succeeded in satisfying them, despite the energetic motion of his figures. This had, admittedly, led to some restraint on the artist "not to be as bold a colorist as he characteristically is." The critic found the *Heliodorus* a great work, even compared to Raphael's. In conclusion, he attempted to answer the question as to why Delacroix had suffered a check in popularity: "M. Delacroix has not been understood in France because he has come after David, an accidental cause, and because he is a colorist, a fundamental cause."[9] The French are essentially rationalists, their characteristic art being "that of the word."

An article by Georges Duplessis (1834-1899, a writer on French art, especially engravings), appearing in *Les deux mondes, illustration religieuse* of January 1862, constituted practically a total criticism of the murals, which Duplessis considered neither religious nor monumental nor—quoting M. Beulé the *Ingriste* as an authority on mural decoration—adapted to the architecture.[10] At Saint-Sulpice, Delacroix is not even successful in his own terms, for his work lacks verve and vitality. The angels of the *Heliodorus* are incorrect anatomically; the shepherd on foot who clambers up the mountain in the *Jacob* should have unequal chiaroscuro effects on his legs since one is in light and the other in shadow, whereas they are equally lighted in the painting. The artist, weak in draftsmanship, falls far short of great colorists like Rembrandt, Rubens, Veronese, and Titian, who could draw excellently. (As a reference for this point, he cited Charles Blanc's *Grammaire des arts du dessin*, which states

that one must unite color to drawing in order t produce good painting.)

On January 18, 1862, Léo de Bernard's article ap peared in *Le monde illustré*. He noticed that th chapel receives daylight from the south, "which perhaps a bit harsh, but which lets one perceive th details of treatment *(facture)* and which seems th preferable to the softened light of the colored win dows that alters the tone and effect of the painting in the other chapels." After praising Delacroix work for its conception and technique, he single out the landscape of the *Jacob* as "the most admir able we've ever seen," and concluded: "Far be from us to declare that other tendencies are bad. but we believe that of all contemporary painter M. Eugène Delacroix is the one whose personalit will stand out the most vividly in the history of ar The Chapelle des Saints-Anges causes us to say sin cerely: 'There is the true painting for eternity.'"

On February 4, 1862, Paul de Saint-Victor (182 1881), a consistent defender of romanticism, pub lished in *La presse* some comments on the chape He considered the *Jacob*, especially its "marvelou landscape," the masterpiece of the chapel, and als praised the group of objects which "magnificentl decks out the foreplane of the painting." He com pared the *St. Michael* (which he found the least suc cessful) and the *Heliodorus* to the correspondin works of Raphael with their simple perfection. "B uniting the old law to the new, and the temple to th basilica, he [Raphael] stamps the scene with the sea of eternity. However," he continued, "it would b unjust and puerile to demand of the *Heliodorus* i Saint-Sulpice the admirable logic, the moral unity the eloquent and pure style that characterizes th fresco in the Vatican." Delacroix's style is differen one of "movement and color." The angels strangel borne on the air remind him of Tintoretto's *St. Mark* There are defects in the *Heliodorus*: "The horse ha

---

8. I do not know whether Delacroix saw this article before his death in 1863, but a letter of January 24, 1862 to Philippe Burty indicates that he still had not seen it then: "Charles Blanc told me that there was to appear in his journal a drawing of one of the paintings of the Chapelle des Saints-

Anges; I have not heard anyone speak of it."

9. Chesneau had already discussed the coldness and austerity of David's school.

10. Beulé's *Cours d'archéologie. La peinture décorative et le grand art*, Paris, 1860, 12-13, attacked

Delacroix's qualities as an artist, even denyin; that his color was any more "a creation" tha that of Ingres or Flandrin, whose color had onl "less seduction" than Delacroix's. Beulé wa *secrétaire perpétuel* of the Institute from 186: on.

ot the ideality of his role" and should be more ashing and supernatural: "I don't like his iron-ray tonality; painted in a bright color it would have ecome the luminous center which the painting cks." If the details are faulty, there is a "great fect of the ensemble" and an effective contrast between the disorder below, where Heliodorus lies, nd the calm of the sanctuary above. On the whole, ainting large works enhances Delacroix's stature: Large murals, there are his arenas; there's where e rules triumphantly, and by this standard will posrity judge him."[11]

The March 1, 1862 issue of the *Gazette des Beaux-Arts* contained an article by A. Gruyer on the muals of H. Flandrin in the nave of Saint-Germaines-Prés, which referred in passing to Delacroix's hapel.[12] The article bewailed the loss of the "golden ge" of Italian mural painting and its replacement y wretched contemporary art, which breaks "the violable unity of God's temple." In this connection e pointed to Delacroix's chapel: "There is a sancary dedicated to the Holy Angels, where the messengers of the Most High, instead of reflecting on a eam of infinite beauty, agitate themselves like maden, with faces of an ugliness that the old masters vould not even have put on madmen." In a note to is remark he added: "As to M. Eugène Delacroix, am far from denying him some high qualities that ake a painter a master....But aside from the fact at M. Eugène Delacroix is below par at Saintulpice, he should have understood that in a church isn't above all the eyes that he must charm or azzle, it is the soul that it is necessary to touch by he nobility of the forms and the elevation of the tyle."

On March 15, 1862, the religious painter O. Meron's detailed and hostile critique appeared in *La evue contemporaine*. He found little to praise in the t. *Michael*, the two protagonists being "gauche"

and "too human." Nor did he take seriously the praise of its colors as making the vault disappear.[13] He liked the *Jacob* better, but felt that the still life was introduced only to fill an empty space, that the angel's wings are "leaden," that the tree branches are "more tormented than true," that the figures gesture uncertainly and that their anatomy is poor. Furthermore, Merson's faith was left unsatisfied by the artist's showing "divine force as if ready to succumb beneath the repeated assaults of human force." The general harmony is a bit dull: "Jacob's tunic, among other things, is of a dirty leaden white." Delacroix neglected the "principles of unity" in the *Jacob*: the shadow of Jacob and of the angel project left and are lighted from the right, whereas the trees and the distant hills show an evening light coming from the background, so that the sun sets in the background and rises in the foreground. Merson considered the *Heliodorus* the most important and deservedly the most praised of the three; however, it doesn't differ much from Raphael's painting, which is superior, even in the differences (e.g. the innovation of having Onias gesture in surprise at the scene he witnesses, as compared to Raphael's "more profound idea" of having the High Priest remain devoutly absorbed, unaware of the miraculous response to his prayers).[14] In general, Delacroix's admirers are wrong to compare the two artists, for Delacroix's good qualities (e.g. richness of color) are of the second order and "satisfy pure sensualism, paganism of thought, but nothing more." Able to "charm the eyes" and fulfill the conditions of art for art's sake, he cannot do so for sacred art, which requires emotions perfected in the soul. The arts that try to persuade and appeal to the soul are eternal, those which appeal to the senses can lead to "paroxysm" and are "ephemeral." The *Heliodorus*, with its variety and richness of tones, is "a feast, a joy for the eyes," with its surprising animation, free-

dom from exaggerated or opaque shadows. It is seductive but undisciplined, for the "colors hardly seem fixed to the wall, but to fly." The ultimate effect of the work is disquieting to the eye, irritating, in keeping with Delacroix's disposition to produce "moral suffering" by an "unusual exaggeration": "the grimaces of expressive muscles, contortions in the gestures, morbid tones, deformity of models and contours...a hatched and incorrect execution...excite painful sensations, difficult to support." Delacroix's nervous and impressionable temperament prevent his being a good religious painter. "What does he want above all? To impress on his works his personality....Doubtless he flees from banality, but he understands by banality beauty, style, calmness of execution...serenity." Delacroix had to fail at Saint-Sulpice for he could not embrace "the cult against which his whole life has been only one long combat."

On April 1, 1862, there appeared in *La revue des deux mondes* a provocative review by Louis Vitet (1802-1873, writer, inspector of historic monuments after 1830) which, with an irony some missed, alternated criticism and praise of the murals. Delacroix's angels are not ministers of hope and charity—as they should be—but of struggle and punishment. In the *St. Michael* the artist made the mistake of measuring himself against the incomparable Raphael, adding nothing but a landscape and some accessories. Raphael's St. Michael (from the larger painting in the Louvre attributed to the master) crushes his enemy, whereas Delacroix's "flies in the air like a bird, like a balloon...and gently grazes his adversary on the shoulders." Delacroix missed the chance to make a work suited to his flair by placing the combat in the clouds rather than near earth. The versions of the *Heliodorus* by the two artists are also compared, and here Vitet, while criticizing the lack of perspective in Delacroix's painting, praised its

---

1. Delacroix liked Saint-Victor's article despite its qualified praise and wrote him a letter on February 17, 1862: "I'd like to thank you for your warm and very kind article; it gives me immense pleasure, especially in the state of weariness in which I find myself...."

12. A. Gruyer (1825-1909) collaborated with Charles Blanc on the *Gazette des Beaux-Arts* after 1858.
13. Cf. Gautier's review of September 1, 1861.

14. Merson stated that he drew this analysis of Raphael's painting from Charles Blanc. See *Grammaire des arts du dessin*, 2nd ed., Paris, 1870, 548.

authentic architecture, which in Raphael's painting is "anachronistic," as is the presence of Julius II and his entourage. While his "local color and chronological truth" are in keeping with "religious constructions of the ancient Orient," in the two punishing angels Delacroix went off in trying to improve on Raphael's perfection, so that the angels fly absurdly wingless in the air and are rather strange; besides, they "take a too lively and personal pleasure in the punishment they inflict, as though they obeyed not divine justice but passionate rage." He liked the cavalier, "really an archangel," preferring his calm to the more brutal version of Raphael, but Heliodorus himself "lacks style" *(sans façon)*, although his position on earth reveals the impact of "Jehovah's raging breath," which also agitates the curtains. The soldiers show terror very well but are "ugly." The main value of Delacroix's *Heliodorus* is to help us appreciate Raphael's, e.g. its empty center, which by a stroke of genius separates supernatural and ordinary beings and isolates Onias at the altar, thereby emphasizing his role in evoking the miracle. The *Jacob* reveals Delacroix's greatest gift: his decorative sense. Whereas less imaginative artists might have painted a "quite Oriental site...arid, naked, desolate...Delacroix has felt that opposite his granite columns he needed other columns of at least equal stature and importance. What trees! Everything about them is colossal, the trunks, the branches....What freshness and mystery beside this bank! Is it really Oriental? I do not know, but it is the most poetically biblical landscape we could dream of." However, the brush strokes are a little too violent, these so-varied plants have hard contrasts, and the effect of the whole dominates too much. Jacob's bull-like thrust is not in keeping with the story: the angel was the powerful one and touched Jacob's thigh not as a last resource but because he saw morning approach.[15] Jacob, with his

"Herculean power and shepherd's rusticity," is a bit lacking in nobility, although filled with movement and life. The angel's legs are a "bit heavy" and "his whole person a bit material," lacking in spirituality. But after all, the figures are secondary, accessories to the landscape, which has hardly any "analogues" even in the Italian masters. There is one minor fault, a departure from the text: "It is earliest dawn that the combat should finish, and his painting is illuminated rather like high noon." Also, there is not enough room in the narrow chapel to see the paintings fully; and at a distance the "harmony, transparency and lightness, so carefully arranged in order to connect by their neutral tones...the side walls to the glistening light of the ceiling," show once more the contradictory quality of the artist. "It is the destiny of certain men to be neither criticized nor praised save with passion." Vitet described a conversation he heard between two persons leaving the chapel, one calling the work a "formless sketch," "pure opera painting, not of an artist but of a decorator," the other regarding the chapel as a "work without equal." The critic thought the work comparable to Delacroix's best and that the artist could not have painted otherwise, given his talents. "There is nothing less religious, that is to say, less sober and tempered than the chapel....It signifies life, the enthusiasm and sparkle of an imperishable youth. Youth, that's the key word! Everyone in France has changed in the last thirty or forty years," but he (like Ingres) has remained unchanged, still "the young Romantic of 1828." Certain details, however, reveal that Delacroix's appearance of youth is "deceiving" and that the artist is essentially "decadent."

With regard to Vitet's article, Tourneux, in his *Eugène Delacroix devant ses contemporains*, noted that it "caused a sensation in its time; the author hailed M. Delacroix as 'a master, a true master' at the moment that Ingres's disciples acclaimed him for

his *Jesus among the Doctors.*" The *Revue anecdotique de 1862* remarked: "M. Vitet...has recently published in the *Revue des deux mondes* an article on the Chapelle des Saints-Anges of M. Delacroix which, because of the opinions expressed there, has been much remarked. It was understood that the friends of M. Ingres were keeping from him news of the event, and the praises of 'the man who smells of sulphur' [an epithet with which Ingres once described Delacroix and which resembles a phrase commonly used in Holland between 1838 and 1840 by opponents of romanticism: *désulfurer l'Hippocrène*, according to Paul Van Tieghem, *Le romantisme dans la littérature européenne*, Paris, 1948, 516] had not yet reached the flawless master when M. Ph. Burty, in the *Chronique des arts et de la curiosité* quoted (with obvious joy) the substance of M. Vitet's article." Ingres became so disturbed that he "immediately took to bed with fever." When Vitet, later meeting him, offered to shake hands with him and said, "You are always the master, sir," Ingres replied, "Sir, I am not the only master." M. Vitet retired, slightly blushing. Delacroix himself apparently read Vitet's original text rather than his friend Burty's version of it and found little in it to please him. In a letter to A. Berryer dated April 13, 1862, he wrote: "What the devil forced him to write ...Couldn't he praise Raphael as much as he wanted and leave me in peace? How unkind of him to insist on this parallel, and how hypocritical his praise seem beside his ill-disguised venom! His great compliment is that I am young. Would that God could take away the years these unhappy criticisms have added to my life! He believes me still in 1825; it is thus that Delécluze treated me at that time. At this moment of my life and career the case is more serious...."[16] Evidently Vitet himself had some misgivings about the article, for when it was reprinted (in L. Vitet, *Etudes sur l'histoire de l'art*, Paris, 1864, III,

15. Actually, there is an important tradition to support Delacroix's interpretation. See, for example, Louis Ginzberg, *Legends of the Bible*, Philadelphia, 1956, 186-87, and the same author's *Legends of the Jews*, Philadelphia, 1913, I, 384-88.

16. Delacroix's old friend Berryer was also a friend of Vitet's. Delacroix's irritation with Vitet for his ironic reference to "youth"—a term of praise among the Romantics—is understandable. Cf. Célestin Nanteuil, the discouraged Romantic's exclamation in 1843, "Il n'y a plus de jeunesse" (cited in Rosenthal, *Du romantisme*, 173).

9-92), he added a postscript regretting that he had discussed incompletely the deceased artist's many-sided talent, and expressing the hope that he would write again on the art of this "fécond et puissant esprit." Delacroix became acquainted with the critic's writing through an article which the artist liked so much that he quoted from it at length in his *Journal* entry of February 3, 1860. Vitet's article, entitled "Pindare et l'art grec," was—like his critique of Saint-Sulpice—published in the *Revue des deux Mondes*.[17] Delacroix underlined a passage in the article about the nature of masterpieces, which at first surprise the world, then are accepted generally and finally lower the world's estimate of those lesser works that preceded them.[18]

On April 25, 1862, F. Boissard wrote for *Le correspondant* an article comparing the religious painting of Hippolyte Flandrin and Delacroix. He spoke first of the unhappy state of religious painting in nineteenth century France. The most important works are to be found, not in the Salons, but in the churches, hence his interest in the murals of Flandrin in Saint-Germain-des-Prés and of Delacroix in Saint-Sulpice. Flandrin's decoration emphasizes line and, while lacking brilliance, possesses religious feeling, whereas Delacroix's, while lacking religious feeling and making errors of anatomy and perspective, has brilliance, movement, color and light. He criticized the architecture of the *Heliodorus*, which detracts from a composition "not lacking grandeur: The grand staircase is faulty. Four columns support it and the last two should evidently be in the same plane, which they are not. Eight steps bypass the column and are supported by forces unknown to the present time....The eye, used to the laws of perspective, perceives that space is lacking between the two columns that cut the middle of the painting." In the *Jacob* the critic admired the gesture of the angel touching Jacob's thigh, which "sums up

the whole scene," whereas he found the anatomy of Jacob's back anatomically incorrect. In the *St. Michael* he noted critically that Lucifer is "thrown down, before St. Michael has struck him with his lance." Despite their faults, he found merits in the murals which, however, do not move us emotionally like the paintings of Flandrin, "who succeeds in moving us only because he is himself moved and interprets ideas which he loves. His faith kindles and vivifies his imagination." Like the religious art of Ingres, that of Flandrin derives, "by logic and necessity," from the Italians.

After this cluster of reviews within the year of the chapel's completion, detailed studies of the chapel became very infrequent, although passing references occurred in articles on Delacroix's work as a whole. The book of A. Cantaloube, published in 1864, *Eugène Delacroix. L'homme et l'artiste*, emphasized the ill effects of Delacroix's lack of faith upon his religious art. Delacroix gave his *Heliodorus* an interest that was thrilling (*palpitant*) but "thoroughly mundane. If Heliodorus' punishment was painted by Delacroix with too human a fury (which makes us feel even more strongly the contrast with Sanzio's supreme interpretation), let us repeat that our great colorist has quite forgotten the *biblical* ferocity in the heart of the Gospel itself. He is modern, he agitates, touches, moves...." His powerful types at Saint-Sulpice are human, even brutal, and they "make us [envisage] Delacroix as the painter of moving dramas, and that he hasn't within him the feeling for divine or mysterious things."

This same attitude toward Delacroix's religious painting was expressed by two writers later the same year in their reviews of the great posthumous exhibition at the Boulevard des Italiens. Charles Gueullette, author of books on miscellaneous subjects, wrote in "Eugène Delacroix. A propos de l'exposition du Boulevard des Italiens," *Les Beaux-Arts.*

Revue de l'art ancien et moderne, 9, No. 8, 1864, 225-28, that "...his religious paintings are skillful studies; there is only one thing lacking, religious feeling. If we admire the *Jacob Wrestling with the Angel* or the *Heliodorus Driven from the Temple*, it is surely not from the Catholic point of view." The archaeologist Alfred Darcel, also writing on the "Exposition de Eugène Delacroix au Boulevard des Italiens," criticized Delacroix's system of hatching and his limitation to human as opposed to "spiritual" feelings. After a passing reference to the *Heliodorus* and the *Jacob*, he commented that Delacroix, who is "too faithful to modern poetics, willingly replaces feeling by action."

Following the great event of the Delacroix sale of February 1864, which brought to public view for the first time much of the artist's work, L. Lagrange—perhaps the only one of his contemporaries to consider the relation of the drawings to the finished painting—wrote in an article in *Le correspondant* on March 25, 1864: "Anyone believing that the idea of beauty was unfamiliar to the painter of the *Pietà* would be deceived. The preparatory drawings for the *Heliodorus* contained some curious information on this subject. We recognized among these drawings several studies of an angel on horseback. At first Delacroix had made him terrible and fatal, eye dilated, the mask of Hamlet beneath the helmet of Othello. It is by successive corrections that Delacroix brought him to the state we see him in, an elegant and pure youth. Likewise, to take a different example, the angel's horse at first advanced quite simply at a trot, the right leg raised and rounded. At the last moment Delacroix decided to stiffen the suspended leg, in order to paint the hesitation of the animal which senses that it is crushing a living body (an astonishing gesture which a reader of Longinus would have little difficulty classifying sublime)."

17. Vitet's article is dated "1er mars 1860" by Delacroix, according to Joubin, an evident anachronism, since Delacroix's entry is dated "3 février" (1860). Actually the article is dated February 1, 1860, and therefore does not contradict the date of Delacroix's entry. Since I have not checked the original manuscript of the *Journal* on this point, I can't say whether the artist or Joubin made the error.

18. Delacroix was probably applying Vitet's remarks to his own work in comparison with that of the old masters.

Henri du Cleuziou's *L'oeuvre de Delacroix*, published in 1865, emphasized the aspect of the artist's lifelong struggle, the "love of combat" which ultimately was transmuted to a "love of peace" when he came to know his own strength. "Still, let one even give him angels to depict, those gentle emblems, so pure, calm and peaceful, and he will only see in them a story of battle" (as in the paintings at Saint-Sulpice).

In 1868 the Abbé Hurel (Manet's friend and sympathizer) published his book on contemporary religious art and mentioned Delacroix's decoration at Saint-Sulpice, with its "appearance of mosaic or of an overloaded palette (as a caricaturist might see it)." He pointed out that "all things being equal, the school of line and moderate color...is proper for works of Christian art. Christianity is pure and calm," qualities he found in the art of Flandrin. However, the "pages of biblical history executed by Delacroix at Saint-Sulpice" have value of another sort, as remarkable documents of "the time in which we live.... Does it not reflect this ardent democracy of which the Church itself must henceforth take account and which invades the sanctuary little by little? If one were to efface Delacroix's fresco (as some have dreamed of doing), then this expression of present-day social customs would have disappeared." He concludes this discussion of Delacroix's chapel with a touch of irony (not necessarily directed against the artist): "After all, the sentiment of piety does not reign exclusively in Christianity." In another place he noted that Delacroix, painter of the *Dante and Virgil in Hell* and the *Massacre of*

Scio, stamps his personality on the Saint-Sulpice murals. His religious sentiment is present and has to do with punishment of intruders and of the devil by guardian angels. Hurel (like Lavergne before him) found a parallel between the Apollo ceiling and the *St. Michael*; Apollo becomes St. Michael and the Python becomes Lucifer. In general, Hurel deplored the low quality of Christian painting in France and found the best contemporary painting in the genre to be that of German Catholics such as Cornelius, Overbeck and Muller.

After the opening of the chapel in 1861, the noisy pros and cons of critical opinion about Delacroix's murals at Saint-Sulpice were hushed, and the general public even in Paris ignored them.[19]

From the late 1860's on, discussions of the murals centered largely around two major issues: their value as compared to earlier masterpieces and their contribution to modern art, especially to Impressionism. The division of contemporary critical opinions about the murals corresponds to the diversity of technical and stylistic influences in them, and opposing critics accordingly made different judgments on the contrary qualities of novelty and convention involved in these paintings. At first, evaluations of Delacroix's art in general depended on an association of the artist with romanticism through his dramatic and exotic subject matter. His color techniques seemed only to intensify the dramatic effect of his themes, heightening the pleasure of some spectators and aggravating the discomfort of others. But with the passing of Delacroix's generation, few of the most capable artists (but a considerable num-

ber of academic painters) turned to romantic or h[i]storical themes; the rare and complicated subject [of] the *Heliodorus* did not lead to new treatments of [it] in French painting.[20] Some artists still painted ve[r]sions of the *Jacob* but generally gave up Delacroi[x's] interpretation of it as a heroic contest within [an] exotic forest. The murals continued to stimula[te] artists (Redon, Cézanne, Renoir, Seurat, Signac) lo[ng] after their first exhibition, but in details of techniq[ue] rather than for their whole composition or for the[ir] subject matter. These questions fall outside t[he] scope of this study.

Especially to many artists influenced by realis[m,] Delacroix's imaginative subjects seemed irreleva[nt.] It has been well pointed out that "Courbet belon[gs] to a period of transition from the cultured artist [of] historical painting...to the artist of the second ha[lf] of the nineteenth century, who relies on sensibili[ty] alone, working directly from nature or from feelin[g,] an eye rather than a mind or imagination."[21] Courb[et] appreciated Delacroix's talent but referred contem[p]tuously to his angels: "M. Delacroix paints ange[ls.] I don't see angels. Do you?...How am I to jud[ge] a form which represents an imaginary being? H[is] wings make him ridiculous and deformed...."[22] V[an] Gogh, although he admired and copied the work [of] Delacroix, agreed with Courbet's rejection of supe[r]natural beings and extended his disapproval to "[all] those historical paintings that they keep on paintin[g] and painting, by yards and yards...."[23] Indeed, [he] called *Jacob Wrestling with the Angel* "that lan[d]scape by Delacroix."[24]

19. The great exhibitions of Delacroix's works in 1864 (Boulevard des Italiens) and 1885 (Ecole des Beaux-Arts) attracted attention to the easel rather than to the mural paintings. See *Le temps*, November 5, 1890, "Tableaux d'Eugène Delacroix dans les églises de Paris," which says of the artist's paintings at Saint-Sulpice: "Cette oeuvre importante de Delacroix fut accueillie avec froideur, et, actuellement, ces peintures...sont peu remarquées par notre génération...." However, a handful of connoisseurs among the writers, notably J.-K. Huysmans and—somewhat later—Anatole France, continued to admire them. Huys-

mans, writing in 1879, found them rare among religious paintings in not depending on stale formulas. See J.-K. Huysmans, "Le Salon de 1879," in *L'art moderne*, 2nd ed., Paris, 1902, 29. France's book, *La révolte des anges* (1914), contains a chapter with an imaginative reworking of critical opinions about the chapel paintings. This occurs in the argument between Abbé Patouille, who represents a stern religious viewpoint (cf. Merson, Lavergne), and Gaétan, sympathetic to Delacroix's genius (cf. Gautier, Baudelaire). France's own opinion apparently is that "the frescoes of the Chapelle des Saints-Anges,

though derided and insulted when they first a[p]peared, have now become part of the classic tr[a]dition, and are united in immortality with th[e] masterpieces of Rubens and Tintoretto."

20. It was engraved by Doré as a Bible illustratio[n] in a late romantic style dependent on Delacroix[s] version.

21. See Meyer Schapiro, "Courbet and Popul[ar] Imagery," *JWarb*, 4, 1940-41, 181.

22. Quoted in Pierre Courthion, *Courbet raconté p[ar] lui-même et par ses amis*, Geneva, 1948, II, 283.

23. In *The Complete Letters*, New York, 1958, II, 39[,] letter 418.

But realism itself was ardently attacked by Delacroix and by old admirers of romanticism such as Théophile Silvestre who, while lauding Delacroix's poetic imagination, disparaged realism for its "negation of imagination."[25] Charles Blanc, who in his later years felt increasing preference for Ingres over Delacroix, was so antagonistic both to realism and to Impressionism, as examples of the "artistic decadence" of the times, that he bewailed the disappearance of "winged beings such as Delacroix."[26] In this period the theatrical humility of Millet's peasants—not the heroic dramas of Delacroix—drew crowds, a fact that provoked sad reflections in Pissarro. Discussing the crowds he had observed at a Millet exhibition in 1887, Pissarro exclaimed: "They were not so dazzled when they looked at the admirable Delacroix decorations in Saint-Sulpice. What animals! It is heartbreaking!"[27]

Admiration for Delacroix was shared by the Impressionists (Pissarro, Renoir) and by survivors of the romantic era who were violent enemies of Impressionism (Charles Blanc, Th. Silvestre, C. Legentil).[28] In 1911 a defender of Delacroix the Romantic, Paul Jamot, tried to trace the origin of Impressionism ultimately to Delacroix's paintings at Saint-Sulpice through the mediation of Auguste Ravier's romantic landscapes.[29]

The Impressionists wrote little about the murals of Saint-Sulpice but were nevertheless very interested in them. They probably preferred the *Jacob* with its landscape to the *Heliodorus* with its architectural setting for the complicated drama, but studied the brilliantly painted details in the foregrounds of both paintings. They were hardly influenced by Delacroix's great decorations of government buildings, which were too high and too poorly illuminated for study and which were in any case rarely accessible to the public. The murals at Saint-Sulpice attracted the Impressionists by their brightness as compared to the darker tonality of paintings by most of Delacroix's contemporaries and his own early romantic paintings. In this lightening of tonality, and in some aspects of his coloring, as has been suggested in Chapter III, the artist paralleled a general trend in painting leading to the Impressionists; but some writers have exaggerated the influence of the artist on the emergence of the new style. Thus, Théodore Duret, in his preface to an exhibition of Monet's works held in June 1880, reprinted under the title "Claude Monet" in *Critique d'avant-garde* (Paris, 1885), 91-105, emphasized the importance of the chapel decorations as a step toward the *peinture claire* of Monet; J.-K. Huysmans, referring especially to easel painting, claimed in his *Certains* (Paris, 1889) that Delacroix opened the way to the Impressionists; and above all Signac made the artist and his chapel paintings the main starting-point for Impressionist painting in his *D'Eugène Delacroix au néo-impressionnisme* (Paris, 1899). In the twentieth century Rosenthal, *Du romantisme*, 167, asserted that the romanticism of Delacroix and of Chassériau "préparait les voies à l'impressionnisme," and H. Focillon, "Delacroix et l'art moderne," *Revue de l'art ancien et moderne*, January 1930, 195-208, asserted that one can practically find in Delacroix's writings "une esthétique et une technique de l'impressionnisme," a view shared (with sensible qualifications) by L. Johnson, *Delacroix*, New York, 1963. The role of the mural decorations in these and later developments has never been clearly defined,[30] nor has the artist's contribution been properly evaluated in relation to other forerunners such as Théodore Rousseau, who made remarks on color and light in nature sometimes strikingly similar to Delacroix's. While the problem falls outside the scope of this book, my own view, briefly, is that the impact of Delacroix's murals was strongest on the expressive and symbolic styles which replaced the more naturalistic aspect of early Impressionism, and that while the Impressionists admired him as a model of courageous independence and found details of his murals stimulating, they were on a different track from Delacroix's dramatic colorism, deeply rooted in tradition. Nor is it probable that they knew of his insights into the laws of color in nature as first published in Achille Piron, *Eugène Delacroix, sa vie et ses oeuvres*, Paris, 1865, since this limited edition of three hundred copies went exclusively to old friends of the master; and the *Correspondance* was first published in 1880, the *Journal* in 1895.

25. *The Complete Letters*, III, 228, letter 613.

26. For Delacroix's remarks, see *Journal*, September 1, 1859. This entry is "certainly a reply to critics of the Salon of 1859, hostile to romanticism and favorable to realism," as Joubin says in a note to vol. III, p. 231. For Silvestre, see *Les artistes français*, 72. Paradoxically, some details of Delacroix's own work, with their documentary realism and their references to direct perception (as discussed in Chapter III), are closer in spirit to the realists than either of the opposed factions realized.

27. See Charles Blanc, *Les Beaux-Arts à l'Exposition de 1878*, Paris, 1878, 178, 187.

28. In *Camille Pissarro: Letters to his Son Lucien*, ed. John Rewald, New York, 1943, 110.

29. See C. Legentil, M. *Alfred Robaut et l'oeuvre de Delacroix: Salon de 1879*, Arras, 1879, 19. See also Henry Havard, "L'exposition des oeuvres d'Eugène Delacroix," *Le siècle*, March 6, 1885: "Rien n'est plus éloigné ... de ce qu'on est convenu d'appeler l'Impressionnisme que cette puissance de conception arrivant à produire juste l'effet qu'elle veut par une méthode scientifique et rigoureuse." For the romantic critics during the Impressionist era, see O. Reuterswärd, *Impressionisterna inför publik och kritik*, Stockholm, 1952.

29. Paul Jamot, *Auguste Ravier. 1814-95*, Lyon, 1911. For Jamot's defense of Delacroix, see his essay "Delacroix" in *Le romantisme et l'art*, Preface by Edouard Herriot, Paris, 1928.

30. Klaus Berger, "Poussin's Style and the XIXth Century," *GBA*, 6th ser., 45, 1955, 161-71, maintained (p. 168) that Delacroix's "pioneer role is revealed ... best in his works of smaller size"; whereas Lee Johnson, in "Delacroix at the Biennale," *BurlM*, 98, 1956, 324-30, asserted (p. 327) that "It is a fallacy to state that Delacroix's easel paintings are of more obvious pictorial value than his large machines and decorative paintings," and pointed especially to Saint-Sulpice, where "it was no chance that Seurat studied." For discussion of possible influences which the murals—among other works by Delacroix—may have had on the works of Cézanne (e.g. the *Heliodorus* on the *Orgy*), see Sara Lichtenstein, "Cézanne and Delacroix," *AB*, 46, 1964, 55-67, and Theodore Reff's letter (with references to articles omitted from Lichtenstein), in Letters to the Editor, *AB*, 46, 1964, 425, and her reply, *ibid.*, 425-26.

BIBLIOGRAPHY OF IMPORTANT SOURCES

Delacroix, Eugène, *Correspondance générale*, ed. André Joubin, Paris, 1935-38, 5 vols.

Delacroix, Eugène, *Journal*, ed. André Joubin, Paris, 1950, 3 vols.

Escholier, Raymond, *Delacroix, peintre, graveur, écrivain*, Paris, 1926-29, 3 vols.

Moreau-Nélaton, Etienne, *Eugène Delacroix raconté par lui-même*, Paris, 1916, 2 vols.

Planet, Louis de, *Souvenirs de travaux de peinture avec M. Eugène Delacroix*, Paris, 1929.

Robaut, Alfred, with comments by Ernest Chesneau, *L'oeuvre complet d'Eugène Delacroix*, Paris, 1885.

Rosenthal, Léon, *Du romantisme au réalisme. Essai sur l'évolution de la peinture en france de 1830 à 1848*, Paris, 1914.

Sérullaz, Maurice, *Mémorial Delacroix*, Paris, 1963.

. . . ., *Les peintures murales de Delacroix*, Paris, 1963.

Tourneux, Maurice, *Eugène Delacroix devant ses contemporains*, Paris, 1886.

INDEX OF NAMES